INVENTOR LAB

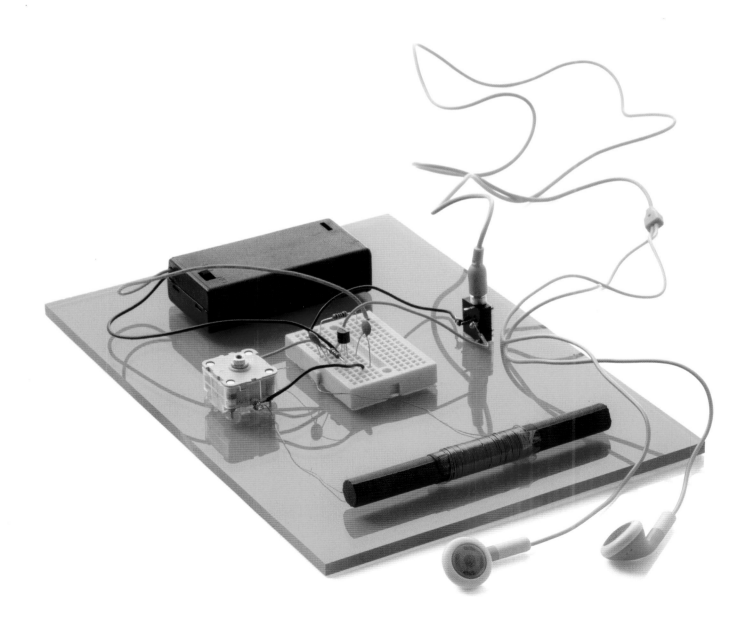

Senior designer Michelle Staples
Senior editor Steven Carton
Designers Daksheeta Pattni,
Anna Pond, Samantha Richiardi
Editors Kelsie Besaw, Alexandra Di Falco

Managing editor Lisa Gillespie
Managing art editor Owen Peyton Jones
Producer, pre-production Jacqueline Street-Elkayam
Senior producer Meskerem Berhane
Jacket designers Tanya Mehrotra, Michelle Staples
Jackets design development manager Sophia MTT
Jackets editor Emma Dawson
Managing jackets editor Saloni Talwar
Jackets editorial coordinator Priyanka Sharma
Jacket DTP designer Harish Aggarwal
Picture researcher Rituraj Singh

Publisher Andrew Mcintyre
Associate publishing director Liz Wheeler
Art director Karen Self
Publishing director Jonathan Metcalf

Writer Jack Challoner
Consultants Stephen Casey, Jack Challoner, Lucy Rogers
Photographer Dave King
Illustrators Adam Brackenbury, Daksheeta Pattni

First published in Great Britain in 2019
by Dorling Kindersley Limited
80 Strand, London, WC2R 0RL

Copyright © 2019 Dorling Kindersley Limited
A Penguin Random House Company
2 4 6 8 10 9 7 5 3 1
001–310503–Oct/2019

A CIP catalogue record for this book
is available from the British Library.
ISBN: 978-0-2413-4351-7

Printed in China

A WORLD OF IDEAS:
SEE ALL THERE IS TO KNOW

www.dk.com

INVENTOR LAB

BRILLIANT BUILDS FOR SUPER MAKERS

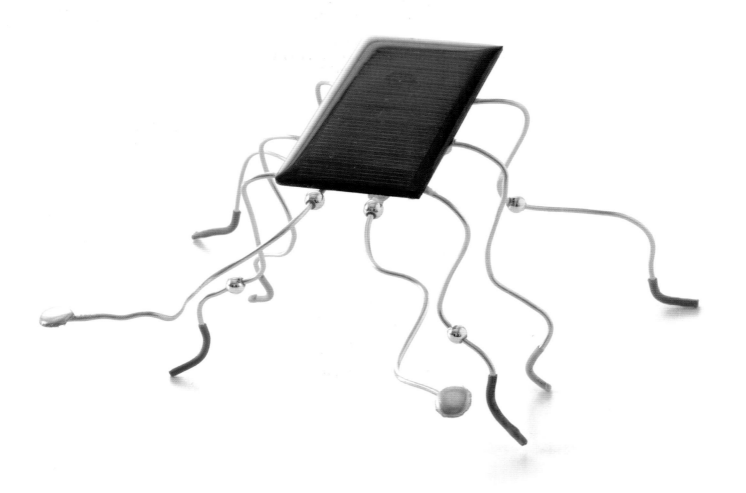

Contents

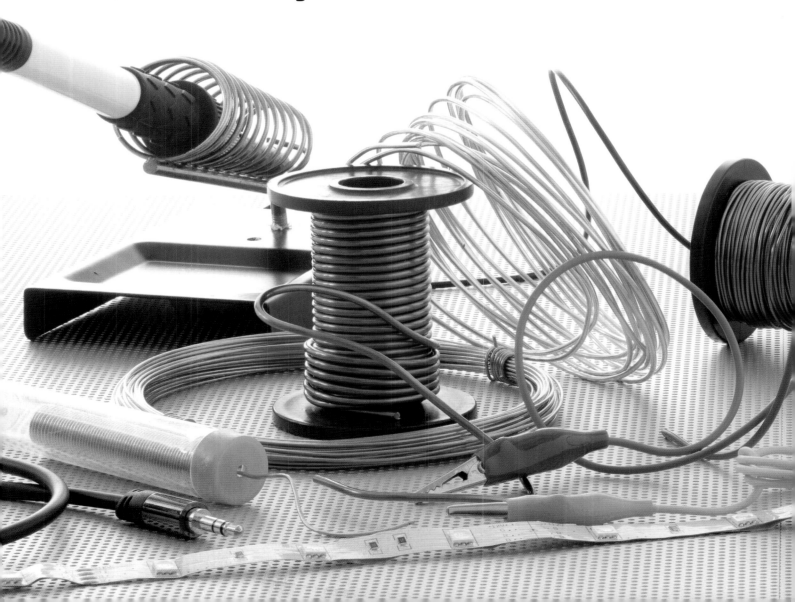

This symbol alerts you to safety issues when making a project. Refer to pp.8–9 for more information on how to do things safely, to avoid harming yourself or those around you.

This symbol alerts you to a particular skill you need for this part of the project, with a page number reference on where to find help with it.

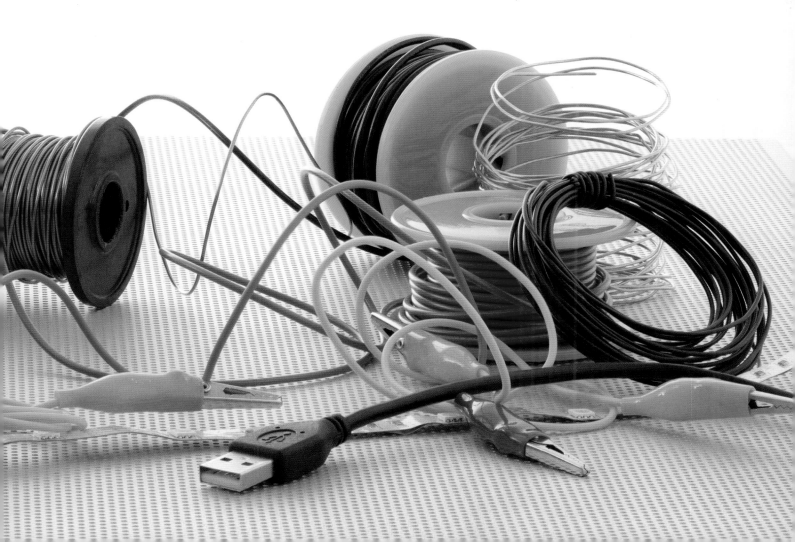

Foreword

Cardboard, sticky tape, and imagination are usually the first steps for makers. But there comes a time when you want to make things that can do a little bit more. This book helps to give you the skills and inspiration for a journey into the world of making, and inventing, really exciting things!

I have always loved to make things. As a child I would happily spend my days working through instructions and building various projects. Not all of my early projects were a huge success – but I always had great fun creating them, and the things I learned on one project, I transferred to the next one.

I would have loved this book as a child – firstly because of the experience of making the projects, but secondly as a result of the challenges they throw up, and the solutions I would have needed to find.

What happens if I use a green LED rather than a red LED? If I don't have double-sided sticky tape, would glue work? Why do LEDs have voltage limits (answer: because if you put too much current through one, it makes a pfffft noise and stops working, which is why we use resistors!). How can I make my project faster or slower or louder or quieter? What happens if I make the wires longer?

Asking, and answering, countless questions such as these is the best way to learn how to create.

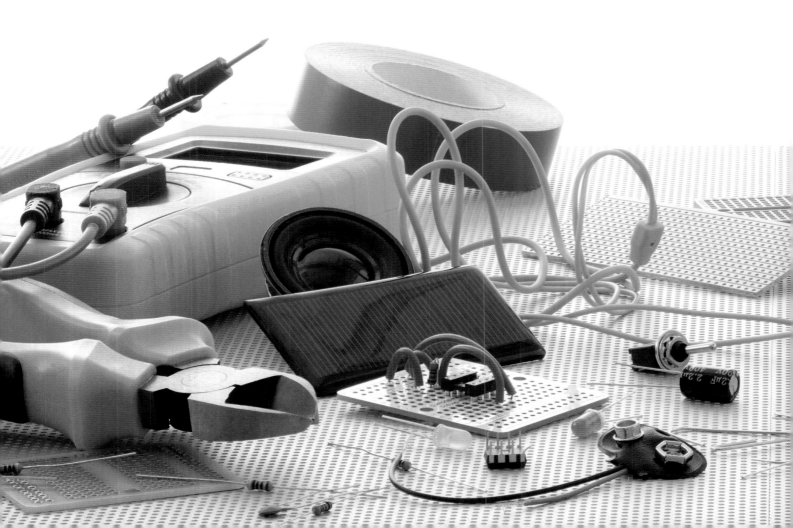

This book gives projects, but more importantly, inspiration, for everyone. The beginner can make the projects, and then when they are made, they can be played with, adapted, sometimes combined, and their limits discovered, and perhaps even overcome. This is precisely the point where "following instructions" changes to "inventing" – and is where the fun really begins and the magic happens!

My ability to create and imagine, to play and have fun, are fundamental in the work that I do as an inventor, an engineer, and a problem solver. And it all started by making projects just like these.

Lucy Rogers

Lucy Rogers

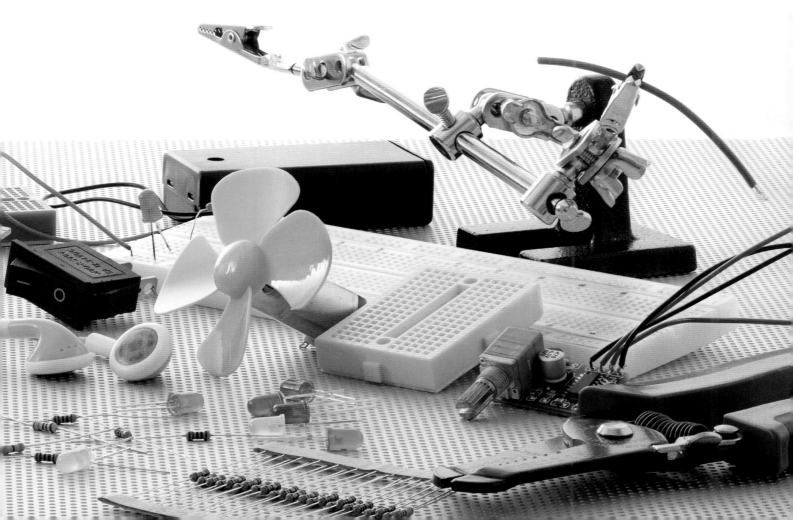

Staying safe

There are lots of exciting projects in this book. We want you to try all of them, and to have fun, but we also want you to stay safe. Read through the general safety tips on these pages before you try any of the projects.

Manufacturer's guidelines

It is always important to read the guidelines that the manufacturers of various tools, components, and safety-wear items include with their products. They aren't all the same, and the things you use might be slightly different from the ones we have used. Ask an adult if you are unsure about anything.

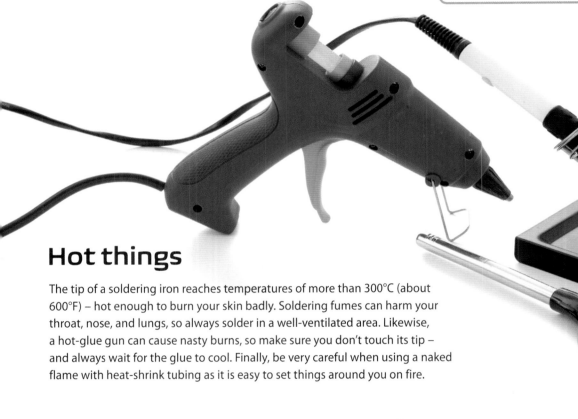

Hot things

The tip of a soldering iron reaches temperatures of more than 300°C (about 600°F) – hot enough to burn your skin badly. Soldering fumes can harm your throat, nose, and lungs, so always solder in a well-ventilated area. Likewise, a hot-glue gun can cause nasty burns, so make sure you don't touch its tip – and always wait for the glue to cool. Finally, be very careful when using a naked flame with heat-shrink tubing as it is easy to set things around you on fire.

Sharp things

The majority of these projects require you to cut and puncture things. Take extra care with scissors, utility knives, saws, and drills as their cutting edges can easily slip and cut you. When making holes in materials, keep your fingers and hair clear of the drill bit when using a drill, and the sharp point when using a bradawl.

Safety wear

You should wear safety goggles and a dust mask when soldering, cutting wires, and drilling, to protect your eyes and throat from small bits of solder, wire, or other debris that can fly into the air. It's recommended that you wear cut-resistant gloves for cutting, but also for handling sharp things.

Electrical hazards

The majority of projects in this book involve electricity supplied by batteries. Never put batteries near or in your mouth. Some projects require mains electricity – it is extremely important to check the project instructions carefully and to make sure your wiring is perfect as mains electricity can cause painful shocks and burns, and can even kill you. For both battery and mains-electric projects, disconnect anything that is becoming hot or smoking, before checking your wiring.

Disposing of things

It is very important to dispose of things properly when they are no longer needed. Most of the electronic components you use can be disconnected and reused. Plastic, card, and paper can be recycled, as can dead batteries. Metal blades can also be recycled – most companies offer safe and environmentally friendly ways of doing this, so check before you buy. It is important that none of these things end up in the regular rubbish.

Working environment

Keep your working area clear and clean. Never have food or drink near where you are making projects. If there are younger children or pets in your home, never leave them unattended near hot, sharp, or electrical objects. When finished, tidy your tools, components, and projects away to minimize the chance of injury.

Toolbox

There are some things that are used again and again in these projects, so much so that we call them our "toolbox". They are mentioned briefly in the "you will need" section of each project, but here they are, with a description of each one. It's a good idea to get an actual toolbox in order to store and organize them properly.

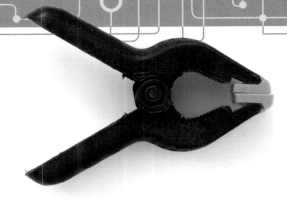

Spring clamp

In this book, we use spring clamps to secure things that need to be drilled or sawed, so they don't move around.

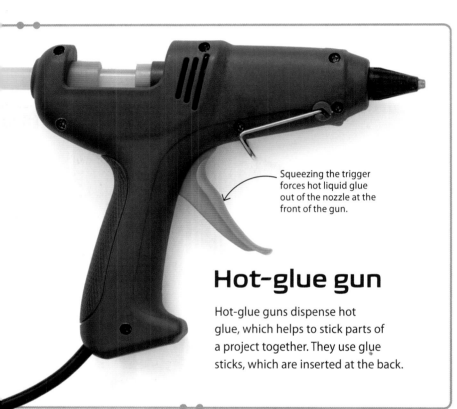

Squeezing the trigger forces hot liquid glue out of the nozzle at the front of the gun.

Hot-glue gun

Hot-glue guns dispense hot glue, which helps to stick parts of a project together. They use glue sticks, which are inserted at the back.

Adhesive putty

Adhesive putty is mainly used in this book to protect work surfaces when you are making a hole in something. You can also use it to hold things in place as you work on them.

Scrap wood

Bits of scrap wood are useful when drilling or sawing to prevent damaging the surface you're working on.

Tape

Sometimes, it's easier to use tape instead of glue to stick things together. In the projects in this book, we use electrical tape, double-sided tape, and double-sided foam tape.

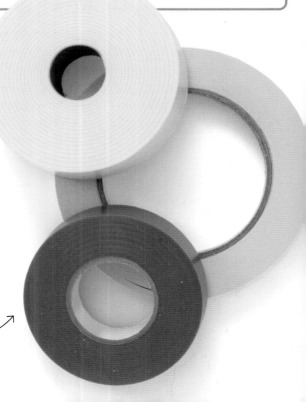

Electrical tape is especially useful for insulating electrical wires.

Utility knife

Use a utility knife to cut through thin plastic or card. The blade of a utility knife is very sharp, so be careful, and always cut against a straight metal edge, such as a metal ruler.

The blade is in sections that snap off when the front one gets blunt. Ask an adult to help you break sections off.

Make sure you use scissors that are clean and sharp.

Cutting mat

When cutting through thin plastic or card with a utility knife, always make sure you use a cutting mat underneath to protect the surface you are working on.

It's best to use a bradawl with a soft-grip handle.

Scissors

Scissors can be used to cut through paper as well as to cut out shapes that don't have straight lines.

Bradawl

The sharp point of a bradawl can make holes in plastic or thin wood. It can also be used to make a small pilot hole to guide you as you begin drilling.

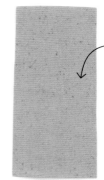

Sandpaper comes in a variety of grain sizes.

Sandpaper

We have used sandpaper to smooth down rough edges, and also to scrape the coating off enamelled copper wires.

Markers or pencils

Most projects involve making marks as a guide for cutting or drilling, so it is a good idea to keep a marker and pencil in your toolbox.

Ruler

Many things in this book need to be measured properly, so you'll need a ruler. We recommend getting a sturdy metal ruler, which has markings for both metric and imperial measurements.

Junior hacksaw

Make sure the teeth on the blade are facing forward.

Use a junior hacksaw to cut through small pieces of wood and plastic pipe. Different types of blades are used for different materials, so make sure you choose the correct type.

Wire strippers

Some wires are coated in a layer of plastic insulation to prevent electricity from flowing where it shouldn't. Wire strippers are used to expose the metal part of the wire so that it can be connected to a circuit.

Drill

A drill uses drill bits to make holes. Drill bits come in many different sizes, and different kinds are used for making holes in specific materials. Ask an adult to help you choose the right drill bit and to help you drill safely.

These drill bits are designed to make holes in wood. They can also make holes in soft plastic.

Wire cutters

In order to prepare wires that need to be connected to a circuit, you will need to use wire cutters to cut the wires to the correct length. Wire cutters can also be used to cut thin pieces of wood.

Pliers

You can use pliers to bend the ends of connecting wires and legs of components, or to shape thick wire. The most useful type of pliers for the projects in this book are "needle-nose" pliers.

Always grip the handle firmly when using pliers.

Third-hand tool

This tool is just what it says it is – a third hand! It can hold components for you, leaving your hands free to do soldering. Some even have magnifying glasses to help you see the small solder joints more clearly.

The red measuring lead determines the positive charge.

The black measuring lead determines the negative charge.

Try to buy solder that doesn't have lead in it.

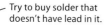

Multimeter

A multimeter is a tool that is used to test circuits and batteries, and to check that components are working.

Keep the dial in the "Off" position when you're not using the multimeter, to conserve the battery.

Soldering iron (and solder)

A soldering iron is used to heat up and melt solder. Solder is an alloy (a mixture of metals) that can be used to join wires and electronic components to make circuits.

The long wires connect the measuring leads to the multimeter.

Components

Every electric circuit is made up of components that control the flow of electric current around the circuit. In this book, you will use many different types of components, and it is useful to understand what they are, how they work, and the things to look out for when you are buying them.

Solar panels come in an array of sizes and shapes, and should be selected with the job they are expected to do in the circuit in mind.

Micro-mini solar panels

Power sources

The most common way to power a circuit is with a battery. Inside a battery, chemical reactions produce electrons and generate electromotive force, which pushes the electrons around the circuit (see "Circuits" on pp.30–31). We also use solar panels in one project to provide electromotive force. The unit of measure of electromotive force is the volt (V).

Solar panels work best with direct sunlight or the beam of a halogen light.

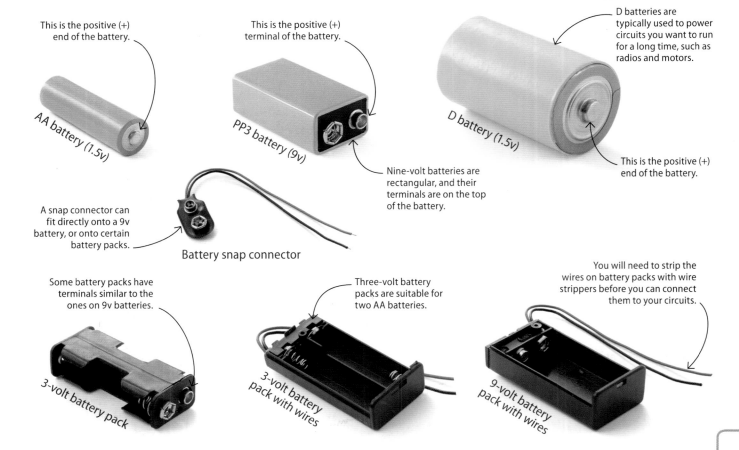

This is the positive (+) end of the battery.

AA battery (1.5v)

This is the positive (+) terminal of the battery.

PP3 battery (9v)

Nine-volt batteries are rectangular, and their terminals are on the top of the battery.

D batteries are typically used to power circuits you want to run for a long time, such as radios and motors.

D battery (1.5v)

This is the positive (+) end of the battery.

A snap connector can fit directly onto a 9v battery, or onto certain battery packs.

Battery snap connector

Some battery packs have terminals similar to the ones on 9v batteries.

3-volt battery pack

Three-volt battery packs are suitable for two AA batteries.

3-volt battery pack with wires

You will need to strip the wires on battery packs with wire strippers before you can connect them to your circuits.

9-volt battery pack with wires

Capacitors

Capacitors are used to store electric charge. When current starts to flow in a circuit, a capacitor begins to charge up – once fully charged, no more current can flow. The unit of capacitance is the farad (F). Most capacitors have a tiny amount of capacitance – normally microfarads (millionths of a farad, μF), nanofarads (billionths, nF), or picofarads (trillionths, pF).

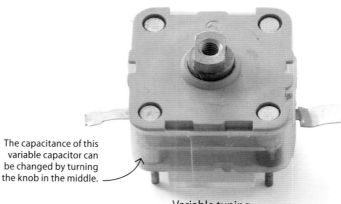

The capacitance of this variable capacitor can be changed by turning the knob in the middle.

Variable tuning capacitor

Electrolytic capacitors have a (+) or (–) marked on them and need to be connected in a circuit with this in mind.

Most capacitors are ceramic capacitors. They are usually coloured orange.

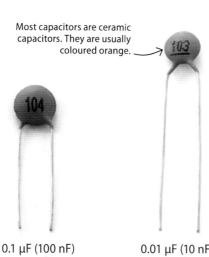

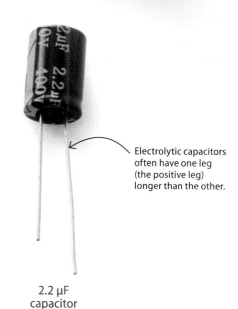

Electrolytic capacitors often have one leg (the positive leg) longer than the other.

0.1 μF (100 nF) capacitor

0.01 μF (10 nF) capacitor

10 μF capacitor

2.2 μF capacitor

1	3	0000
The "1" indicates the first number of the capacitance.	The "3" indicates the second number of the capacitance.	The "4" shows the amount of zeros to add, making this capacitor 130,000 pF.

Reading a capacitor

On some capacitors, the actual value may be written out: for example, 34 nanofarad would be written "34 nF". On most capacitors, however, there are only numbers. The numbers form a code for the capacitance in picofarads (pF). The first two are digits, and the third one is the number of zeros to add. To convert to nanofarads, divide by 1,000.

Resistors

Resistors are used to control the amount of electric current and voltage supplied to different parts of a circuit. They can ensure that a particular leg of a transistor is supplied with the correct voltage, for example, or control how fast a capacitor charges. The value of a resistor is measured in ohms (Ω). One thousand ohms is one kiloohm (kΩ), while one million ohms is one megaohm (MΩ).

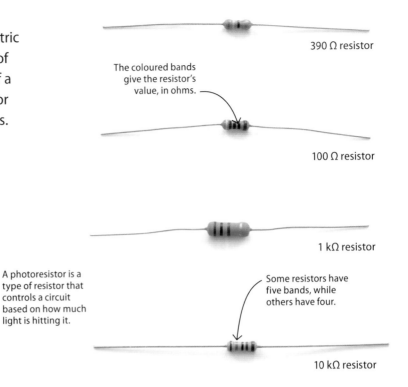

390 Ω resistor

The coloured bands give the resistor's value, in ohms.

100 Ω resistor

1 kΩ resistor

A photoresistor is a type of resistor that controls a circuit based on how much light is hitting it.

Some resistors have five bands, while others have four.

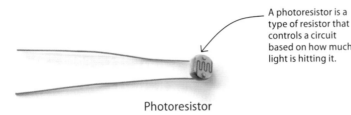

Photoresistor

10 kΩ resistor

Reading a resistor

The diagram to the right shows you how to read the four (or five) grouped coloured bands of a resistor to determine its resistance value. The first three bands are numbers, with the fourth being the multiplier. The separated coloured band on the far right of the resistor tells you how dependable the given value is. In this case, the resistor's bands are yellow, purple (or violet), and black – which gives the number 470. The fourth band is red, which means it's 470 multiplied by 100 Ω, which equals 47,000 Ω (usually written as 47 kΩ). The final band is the tolerance, which is brown, meaning the resistor's true value is within 1% of the 47 kΩ reading.

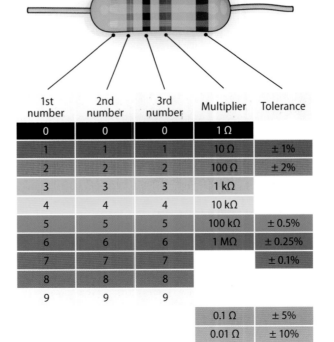

1st number	2nd number	3rd number	Multiplier	Tolerance
0	0	0	1 Ω	
1	1	1	10 Ω	± 1%
2	2	2	100 Ω	± 2%
3	3	3	1 kΩ	
4	4	4	10 kΩ	
5	5	5	100 kΩ	± 0.5%
6	6	6	1 MΩ	± 0.25%
7	7	7		± 0.1%
8	8	8		
9	9	9		
			0.1 Ω	± 5%
			0.01 Ω	± 10%

Transistors

Most transistors have three terminals – emitter, base, and collector. When a small amount of current flows into the base, it allows electrons to flow from the emitter to the collector (or from the collector to the emitter). A transistor can also act as an amplifier, because the large current flowing between the emitter and collector is a copy of the changes in the much smaller current flowing through the base.

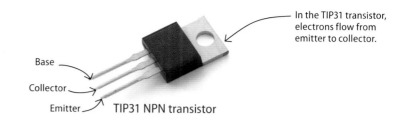

In the TIP31 transistor, electrons flow from emitter to collector.

Base

Collector

Emitter

TIP31 NPN transistor

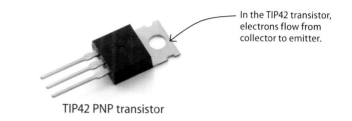

In the TIP42 transistor, electrons flow from collector to emitter.

TIP42 PNP transistor

Speaker and earphones

Speakers, when supplied with varying electric currents, produce vibrations that travel through the air as sound waves. Earphones contain tiny speakers. Piezo sounders can only produce simple sounds, like buzzes or single tones.

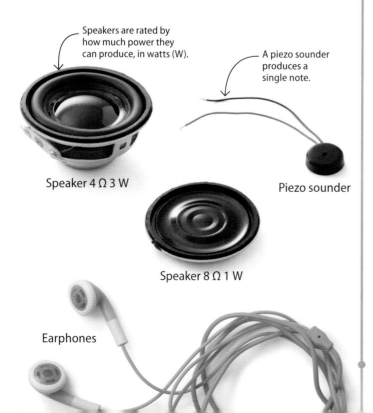

Speakers are rated by how much power they can produce, in watts (W).

A piezo sounder produces a single note.

Speaker 4 Ω 3 W

Piezo sounder

Speaker 8 Ω 1 W

Earphones

Magnet

You are probably familiar with permanent magnets. These always have a magnetic field and a "north" and "south" pole. Electromagnets are coils of wire, normally wound around an object containing iron. They only have a magnetic field when current flows through the coil.

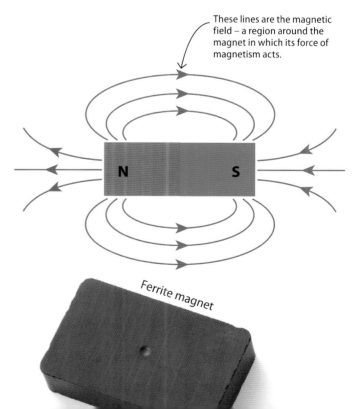

These lines are the magnetic field – a region around the magnet in which its force of magnetism acts.

N   S

Ferrite magnet

Wires

The connections between components are normally made with wires. The wire itself is metal, a good conductor. That means electricity can flow easily (with almost no resistance) through it. Wires are normally covered in plastic or enamel (lacquer), which do not conduct electricity, to prevent short circuits (see p.38).

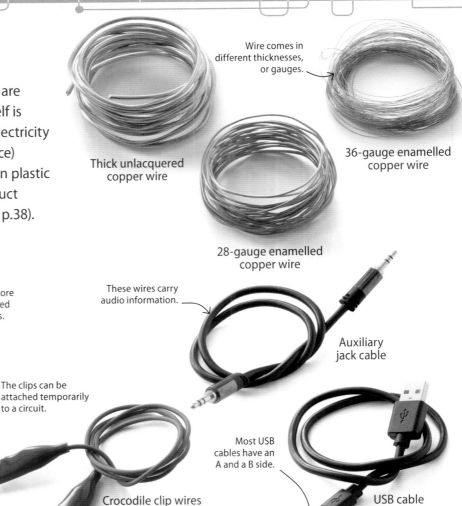

Wire comes in different thicknesses, or gauges.

Thick unlacquered copper wire

36-gauge enamelled copper wire

28-gauge enamelled copper wire

You can use solid-core or stranded insulated wire in your circuits.

These wires carry audio information.

Auxiliary jack cable

The clips can be attached temporarily to a circuit.

Most USB cables have an A and a B side.

Red and black insulated wire

Crocodile clip wires

USB cable

Integrated circuits

Inside complicated electronic devices such as smartphones are several integrated circuits (ICs). These small packages contain ready-made circuits, with transistors, resistors, diodes, and capacitors, all built into a single piece of material. In this book, we use the 555 timer IC, which has eight legs – each with its own function. We also use the TA7642 chip, which is able to pick up AM radio signals.

TA7642 chip

Each leg has a specific function in a circuit.

Always take note of which way the notch in the IC should face in a circuit.

555 timer IC

Motors

All motors convert electrical energy into movement energy. Coils inside the motor's body are pushed around by magnetic forces. Different motors require different voltages, so make sure you use the right one for the project you are working on.

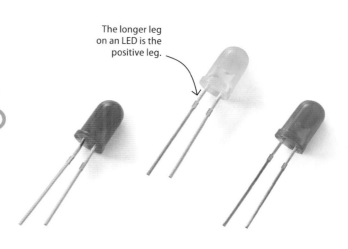

The longer leg on an LED is the positive leg.

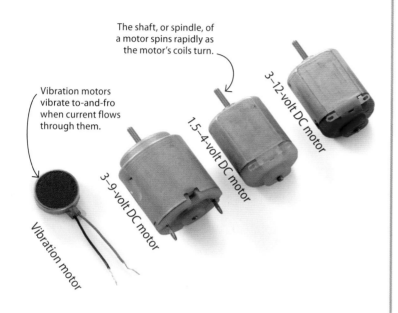

The shaft, or spindle, of a motor spins rapidly as the motor's coils turn.

Vibration motors vibrate to-and-fro when current flows through them.

Vibration motor

3–9-volt DC motor

1.5–4-volt DC motor

3–12-volt DC motor

LEDs

LED stands for "light-emitting diode". A diode is a component that allows electric current to flow in one direction only. It must be connected the right way round in a circuit, so all diodes are marked with a (+) or a (−) sign, or they have one leg shorter than the other. An LED is a diode that produces light when current flows through it.

Single-pole, single-throw (SPST) switch

Switches

A switch is a mechanical device that creates a break in a circuit. When you activate the switch, it opens or closes the circuit, depending on the type of switch it is. "Single-pole, single-throw" switches are the simplest and most common type of switch. They either allow or prevent current to flow.

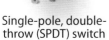

An SPDT switch only allows current through one circuit or another.

Single-pole, double-throw (SPDT) switch

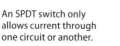
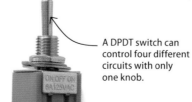

A DPDT switch can control four different circuits with only one knob.

Double-pole, double-throw (DPDT) switch

A button switch only allows current through when the button is pressed.

Tactile button switch

Skills

You are going to be making a lot of very exciting things as you work through this book. It's a good idea to brush up on the basic skills you will need in order to make these projects properly, and also to stay safe. You may need to ask an adult for permission to use tools, and if you encounter any problems when performing these skills.

Cutting things

Scissors are great for cutting paper or thin card, but to make a straight cut through thicker card, you need to use a utility knife. And for cutting wood, plastic, or metal, you will need saws. Whatever you are cutting, mark it out carefully first, using a pencil and ruler. Cutting tools have sharp blades, so you need to measure carefully, keep your work environment clear, and concentrate as you cut.

Utility knife

In order to cut thick card or foam board, you will need to use a utility knife (also known as a craft knife). These knives have extremely sharp blades, so take extra care, and ask an adult if you are unsure about using them. You may want to ask an adult to help you change the blade when it becomes blunt.

Be aware
Wear safety goggles and gloves when cutting, even with a utility knife, as the blade could snap. See "Sharp things" on p.8 and "Safety wear" on p.9 for more tips.

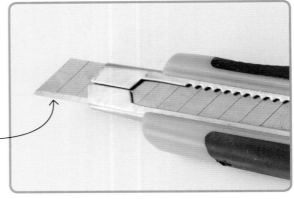

This is the cutting side.

1 Study the blade to see which is the cutting side. Using the wrong side could cause the knife to slip. If the blade is extendable, don't extend it too far as it may wobble or snap.

2 Place the material to be cut on a cutting mat. Line up a straight metal edge, such as a metal ruler, where you want to make your cut. Hold the metal edge down securely in place.

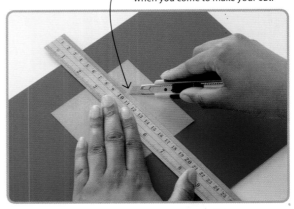

You may find that lightly scoring the material a few times will help when you come to make your cut.

3 Press down firmly on the handle of the blade and pull the knife slowly across the material, at an angle away from your body. Be careful not to go too fast or let the knife slip over the metal edge.

Hacksaw

A hacksaw has a cutting blade stretched across its frame. It can cut through wood, metal, and plastic, depending on the blade you use. When you use a hacksaw, you cut with a backwards and forwards motion, with pressure applied on the forwards stroke. As with any cutting tool, a hacksaw can be dangerous if used incorrectly.

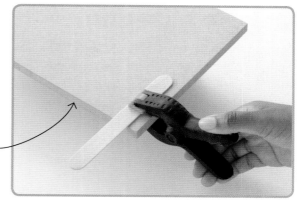

Scrap wood protects your working surface, and also provides a little bit of a ledge to allow you to cut properly.

1 Use clamps or a vice to hold what you are cutting firmly in place. Secure the item you are cutting over the edge of your worktable, or to some scrap wood.

Keep the hacksaw as straight as you can when cutting.

2 Press the blade firmly down and away from you. If you don't have a vice, find a safe way to lean on one end of the item while the other end hangs over the edge of the table.

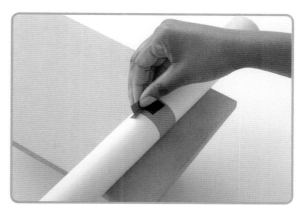

3 If you are cutting pipe (which you need to do in one of the projects), wrap a piece of paper around the pipe and tape it in place. This will give you a flat edge as a guide to saw against.

4 Hold the handle of the hacksaw firmly and angle the saw downwards. Press the blade away and down, keeping the saw in one line. You may need to start slowly in order to create a groove in the pipe.

As the pipe is round, you can't use clamps and may not have a vice that can steady it. Instead, hold the pipe firmly with your free hand.

Using a glue gun

Many of the projects in this book use strong glue dispensed by a hot-glue gun. The glue comes from glue sticks, which are inserted in the back of the gun. When plugged into mains electricity, a heating element inside the gun melts the glue stick. The glue becomes very hot inside the gun, so never pull out a glue stick, and never leave a glue gun plugged in and unattended. You will need to plan your where to work when using a glue gun as most do not have long power cables.

Manufacturer's instructions

Don't forget to check the manufacturer's instructions on how to use their tools (particularly for electrical tools). Each manufacturer makes tools a little differently, and so might include features that make a tool easier to use, or things you need to take into consideration when using that tool.

Be aware
The nozzle and the glue are hot, so don't touch them. If you do, run your skin under icy cold water for a few minutes.
See "Hot things" on p.8 for more tips.

1 Place paper or a work mat onto your work surface to catch any hot glue that might drop by accident. Plug in the glue gun, place it safely on its stand, and wait for a few minutes for the glue to heat up.

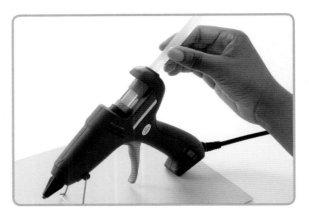

2 Make sure enough glue is loaded into the glue gun. If the stick in the gun is short, simply push another stick in through the hole in the back of the gun. Before starting, make sure the items you are going to glue are clean and dry.

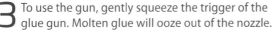

Keeping the trigger pressed will keep the hot glue coming from the nozzle.

3 To use the gun, gently squeeze the trigger of the glue gun. Molten glue will ooze out of the nozzle.

4 Release the trigger once you have applied enough glue. The glue takes about 30 seconds to cool and solidify. Do not touch the glue until it has dried as it can burn you.

Drilling

A drill is a powerful machine that makes holes in things. The part of the drill that makes the holes is the drill bit. There are drill bits specially designed for making holes in wood, plastic, metal, and concrete, so ask an adult to help you select the right kind. Drill bits also come in a wide range of sizes (relating to the width of the drill bit), so that you can be sure to make the hole the right size.

!

Be aware

Make sure you tie back your hair if it is long and secure any loose clothing before drilling. See "Sharp things" on p.8 and "Safety wear" on p.9 for more tips.

This is the chuck.

1 Once you have selected the correct drill bit, insert it into the front part of the drill, called the chuck. Turning the ring at the front of the drill opens and closes the jaws of the chuck.

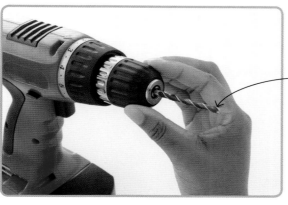

Make sure the drill bit is straight before drilling with it.

2 Twist the ring clockwise to close the jaws around the drill bit. Turn it as far as you can to make sure the drill bit is securely held in the chuck. You can remove the drill bit by turning the ring anticlockwise.

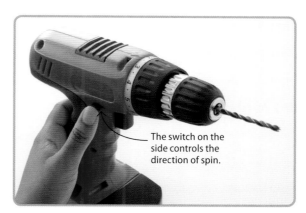

The switch on the side controls the direction of spin.

3 With the drill bit secured, you are ready to begin drilling. Make sure your drill bit spins clockwise when viewed from behind the drill. Flip the switch on the side if it's spinning anticlockwise.

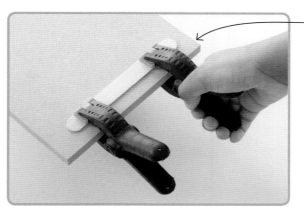

Use scrap wood underneath your item so you don't drill into your work surface.

4 Use clamps or a vice to secure the item you are drilling. This will stop it spinning around and will free your hands to concentrate on the drilling.

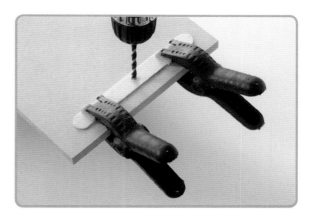

5 Place the drill bit where you want to drill. Squeeze the trigger, and press the drill bit firmly down. Make sure you keep the drill straight so you don't drill a crooked hole.

Using a bradawl

A bradawl can be used to make a guide, or pilot, hole in something you want to drill. It can also be used when you need to make a hole in a flexible material, like a plastic bottle or box.

Be aware
The tip of the bradawl is very sharp, and can easily puncture and tear skin. Keep it away from your eyes at all times. See "Sharp things" on p.8 for more tips.

1 Place some adhesive putty underneath the material in which you want to make your hole. Push the bradawl through the material, twisting to and fro, until it reaches the adhesive putty.

2 If you can't use adhesive putty, carefully hold the material, with your fingers away from where you are making the hole. Push the bradawl, twisting it to and fro, until it comes through the other side.

Preparing wires

Wires have a layer of plastic insulation. To make a connection to a circuit, the end of the insulation needs to be stripped off to reveal the metal wire inside. Normally, you just need to strip about 1 cm (³⁄₈ in) off the end.

Be aware
Stranded wires can be quite sharp, and can puncture the skin. Be careful when using sharp things to cut wires. See "Sharp things" on p.8 for more tips.

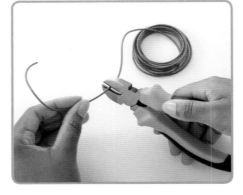

1 First, cut the wire if necessary with wire cutters. Some wire-stripping tools have a cutting blade, but you can also use a pair of wire cutters, scissors, or pliers.

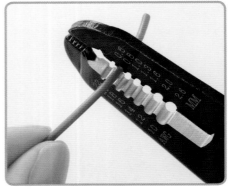

2 Put the end of the wire through the open jaws of the wire-stripping tool. The tool has lots of different-sized holes. Find the one that matches the wire by gently squeezing the handles together.

3 Now squeeze the handles together more firmly and pull the wire away from the wire-stripping tool. The insulation should come away cleanly.

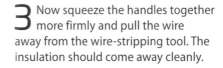

Before cutting or stripping a wire, make sure the wire is not connected in a live circuit. See "Electrical hazards" on p.9 for more tips.

Soldering

A soldering iron is one of the most essential tools when making electric circuits. It is used to melt solder, which is a metal alloy (a mixture of metals). When the solder cools, it solidifies to create a strong bond between wires and components. Because it is made of metals, solder conducts electricity. Make sure the solder you use is designed for electrics and not plumbing.

Always be aware of the position of the flex, so you don't accidentally pull the soldering iron off the table.

1 When you are doing any soldering work, make sure you sit at a bench or put down paper as droplets of solder can fall off and damage the table.

! The fumes produced during soldering can irritate asthma, so don't get too close – and make sure the room is well ventilated. See "Hot things" on p.8 for more tips.

When you're not using it, place the soldering iron safely back in its stand.

Be careful not to let your skin come into contact with the hot soldering iron.

Set your soldering iron to the lowest temperature setting.

2 Place the soldering iron in its holder and turn it on. It will get very hot within a few minutes, so take care! Make sure you wear safety goggles because hot solder can spit.

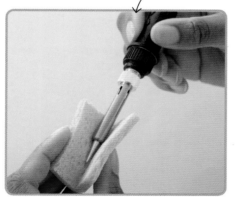

3 Before you start soldering, clean the tip of the soldering iron on a wet sponge – some soldering iron stands have a sponge built in. Alternatively, you can buy a bronze sponge specially designed to clean soldering iron tips.

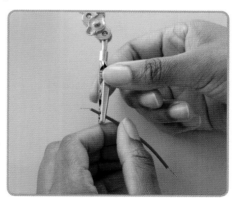

4 It's a good idea to use a third-hand tool to hold the wires or components to be soldered. This allows you to safely hold the soldering iron and solder in each hand while you make your connections.

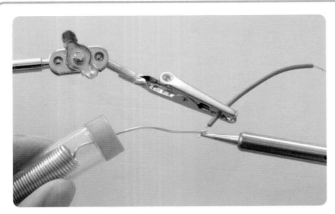

Tinning

It is generally a good idea to cover the parts to be joined with a thin coat of solder, as it helps to ensure the wires will make a good electrical connection. This is called tinning. To do this, place the soldering iron onto the end of a stripped wire or onto the terminal of a component. After about two or three seconds, touch the solder onto the heated wire or terminal, and the solder should flow onto it. It is also a good idea to tin the tip of the soldering iron just before you start soldering to protect it from rusting.

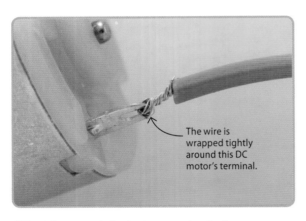

The wire is wrapped tightly around this DC motor's terminal.

5 Make a good physical connection before you solder. If you're attaching a wire to something, twist it firmly around whatever you're connecting it to.

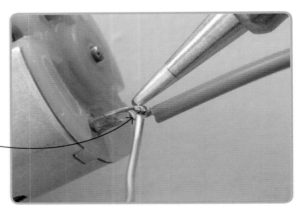

Don't push the solder – just touch it onto the joint and let the liquefied solder flow.

6 Hold the soldering iron against the joint, not the solder. The solder will melt onto the hot joint within a second or two. When it has done so, remove the soldering iron, but keep the joined parts still for a few seconds to let the solder solidify.

Component leg

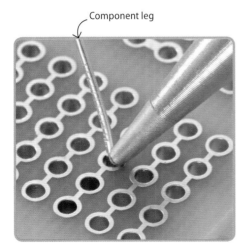

7 When soldering a component to a perforated breadboard, touch the soldering iron to the hole for a few seconds.

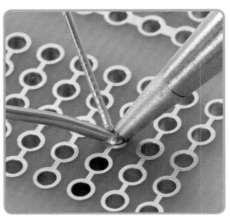

8 Once the hole and the component are hot, touch the solder to the hole.

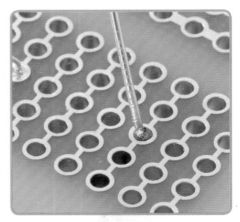

9 The solder will flow around the soldering iron and fill the hole, securing the component leg to the board.

Using heat-shrink tubing

In some of the projects, you will be using heat-shrink tubing. This is a flexible plastic tube that shrinks when you apply heat to it. It is used to cover soldered joints to make sure no other parts of a circuit can touch them. It will also make the joint more robust.

Don't apply the flame for more than a few seconds, and don't hold it too close to the tubing. See "Hot things" on p.8 for more tips.

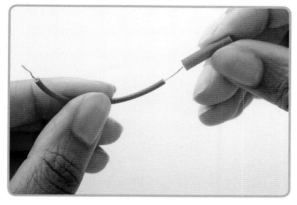

1 Before you begin soldering two wires together, cut the tubing so that it will safely cover the join in the wires. Slip the tubing over one of the wires.

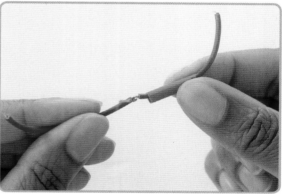

2 When your two wires are soldered, slip the tubing over the solder joint so that it covers it completely.

3 Apply heat for a few seconds with a grill lighter flame. Move the flame slowly around and gradually turn the joint if you can.

Turn the joint around to ensure the tube shrinks evenly on all sides.

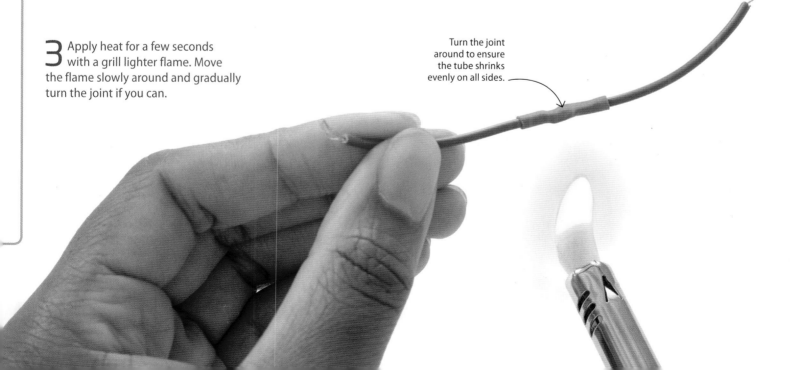

Using a multimeter

A multimeter is a device that can measure voltage, current, and resistance. In the projects in this book, you will only be using it to check that there is a continuous path for electricity to flow through your circuits, or through the components you use. You do this by testing to see if electricity can flow between the two metal prongs. This is very useful for checking if there is a broken connection in your circuit.

This section is used to measure electric current, in amps (A).

The prongs connect to these sockets.

This section is used to measure voltage (V), measured in volts.

This section is used to measure resistance, in ohms (Ω).

Every multimeter is different, so you may need to read the manual if your model is different to this one.

1 Plug the multimeter's red and black measuring prongs into the red and black sockets. If your multimeter's sockets aren't coloured, plug the black lead into "COM" and the red lead into "VΩmA". If your model doesn't have these markings, you may need to search online for its particular layout.

This setting is useful for testing for short circuits, broken wires, or loose connections.

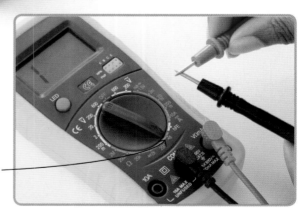

2 If your multimeter has a continuity test setting (the icon looks like a sound wave), turn the dial to it. Touch the measuring prongs together. You should hear a high-pitched noise when they come into contact, which shows that the prongs are working. Next, you will test your circuit.

3 To check if there's a break in a circuit, or if there's a short circuit – in which case, there would be continuity between two parts of a circuit where there shouldn't be – use the continuity setting. In the circuit below, there was no current flowing through the LED, so we carried out a continuity test to see if the breadboard was faulty, as the components were plugged in correctly.

The LED is not lit up because electricity is not passing through it.

Breadboard test

When we carried out this test, the multimeter was silent. This is because it did not detect continuity between the legs of the resistor and the LED. The only possible reason for this is that the breadboard is faulty.

The resistance is very high, which shows there is no continuity between the resistor and the LED.

If the reading is positive, that means the red prong is touching the positive part of the circuit.

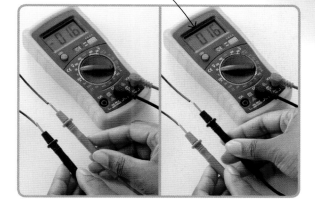

4 If your multimeter does not have a continuity test setting, set the dial to the most sensitive resistance setting. This may be indicated by the word "Resistance" or by the symbol for ohms (Ω). In a functioning circuit, your multimeter should read close to zero.

5 You can use your multimeter to test for polarity in wires – which is positive and which is negative. Click the dial to a voltage setting (V) just above the voltage of the circuit. Touch the prongs to the wires. If there is a minus symbol in front of the number reading, swap the leads.

Electric circuits

All of the projects in this book involve building electric circuits. In each case, electric current flows around a circuit, providing energy to make something happen – such as lighting a lamp or making sound in a loudspeaker. Current can only flow if there is a complete circuit – a path along which the electrons can move.

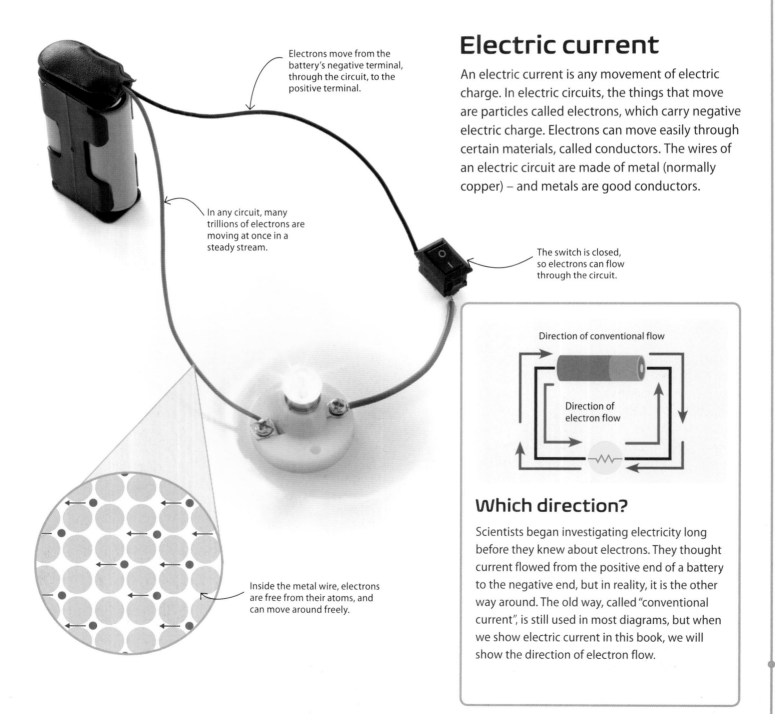

Electrons move from the battery's negative terminal, through the circuit, to the positive terminal.

In any circuit, many trillions of electrons are moving at once in a steady stream.

Inside the metal wire, electrons are free from their atoms, and can move around freely.

The switch is closed, so electrons can flow through the circuit.

Direction of conventional flow

Direction of electron flow

Electric current

An electric current is any movement of electric charge. In electric circuits, the things that move are particles called electrons, which carry negative electric charge. Electrons can move easily through certain materials, called conductors. The wires of an electric circuit are made of metal (normally copper) – and metals are good conductors.

Which direction?

Scientists began investigating electricity long before they knew about electrons. They thought current flowed from the positive end of a battery to the negative end, but in reality, it is the other way around. The old way, called "conventional current", is still used in most diagrams, but when we show electric current in this book, we will show the direction of electron flow.

Voltage, current, and resistance

In order to understand electric circuits, you will need to know about voltage, current, and resistance. To help you grasp what these mean, it helps to imagine an electric circuit as a loop of pipes with water pushed through them by a pump. In this analogy, the pump is a battery, the pipes are the wires, and the water represents the electrons.

Voltage

To produce a current in an electric circuit, there has to be a force on the electrons. That force, called an electromotive force (emf), can be supplied in many ways – for example, by a battery. The greater the emf, the more energy the electrons have, and voltage, in units called volts (V), is a measure of the energy of each electron. In the water analogy, voltage is the pressure the pump produces.

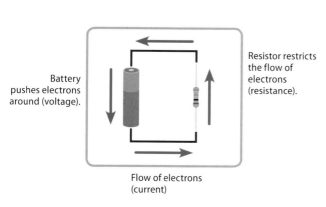

Battery pushes electrons around (voltage).

Resistor restricts the flow of electrons (resistance).

Flow of electrons (current)

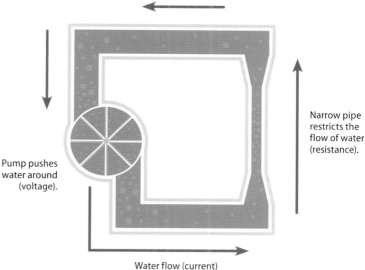

Pump pushes water around (voltage).

Narrow pipe restricts the flow of water (resistance).

Water flow (current)

Current

The current flowing in a circuit is a measure of the number of electrons passing any point in the circuit each second. The greater the voltage and the lower the resistance, the greater the current. Electric current is measured in units called amperes (A), or amps for short. In the water analogy, current is the amount of water flowing per second.

Resistance

Electrons move easily through metal wires – as the wires put up very little resistance to their movement. But most electrical components have some resistance, and the total resistance of a circuit determines the flow of electrons (the current). Resistance is measured in units called ohms (Ω). Resistors are components that have particular resistances – they control current in a circuit. In the water analogy, resistance is the width of the pipes.

Ohm's Law

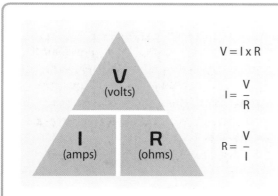

$$V = I \times R$$

$$I = \frac{V}{R}$$

$$R = \frac{V}{I}$$

A rule called Ohm's Law, shown as a mathematical equation, summarizes the relationship between the voltage, resistance, and current in a circuit. The equation states that voltage is current multiplied by resistance; current is voltage divided by resistance; and resistance is voltage divided by current. If you know two of the values, you can work out the third using Ohm's Law. Ohm's Law is useful when designing circuits, as you can use it to quickly find out what components you need to build a working circuit safely.

Series and parallel circuits

In some circuits, the wires and components are connected one after another, "in series". In other circuits, there are branches in the circuit, in which case the wires and components are "in parallel". Most circuits have at least some components connected in parallel.

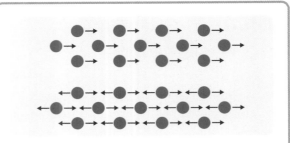

AC and DC

In some circuits, the electrons move in one direction only – this is called direct current (DC, top illustration above). In others, they move backwards and forwards. In that case it is called alternating current (AC, bottom illustration above).

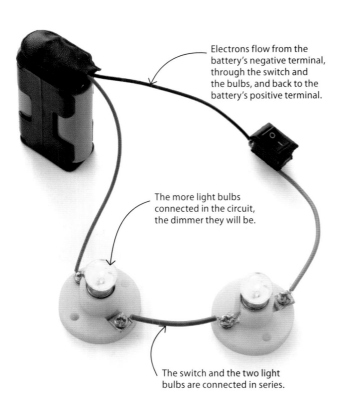

Electrons flow from the battery's negative terminal, through the switch and the bulbs, and back to the battery's positive terminal.

The more light bulbs connected in the circuit, the dimmer they will be.

The switch and the two light bulbs are connected in series.

Series circuits

In a series circuit, there is only one path through which the current can flow. All the electrons pass along the same route. The current in a series circuit is the same throughout the circuit – it is determined by the total resistance of all the components. The energy of the electrons is shared between all the components.

Parallel circuits

In a parallel circuit, electric current can flow through different paths because the circuit branches. Some electrons will go one way, and others, another. The current in each branch depends on the total resistance of the components in that branch – and each branch receives all the energy of the electrons that come that way.

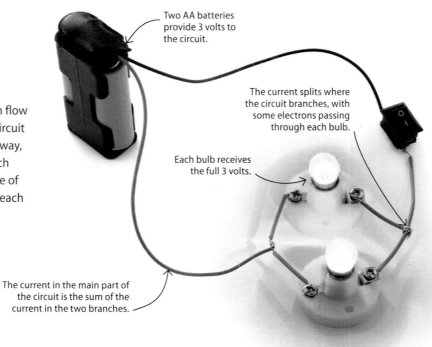

Two AA batteries provide 3 volts to the circuit.

The current splits where the circuit branches, with some electrons passing through each bulb.

Each bulb receives the full 3 volts.

The current in the main part of the circuit is the sum of the current in the two branches.

Circuit diagrams

When electronics engineers are building circuits, they don't draw the battery, wires, and components as they are in real life. Instead, they use diagrams that show clearly how the various parts of the circuit are connected. So that there is no confusion, there are standard symbols for each kind of component, and wires are shown as straight, even if in the actual circuit the wires bend. We have included circuit diagrams for every project on pp.152–155.

9v battery   Switch   Bulb

1 kΩ resistor   LED   Motor

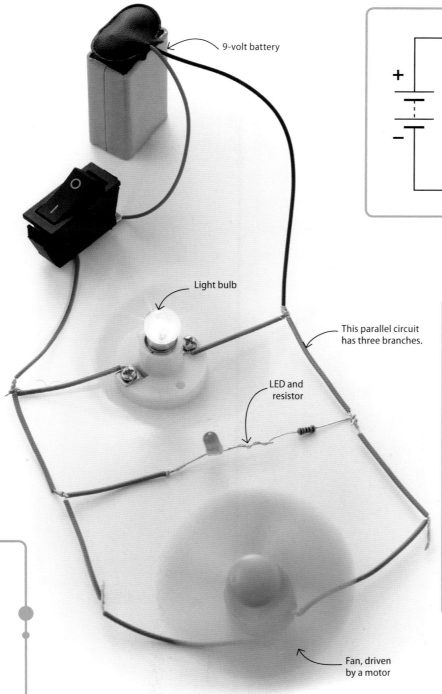

9-volt battery

Light bulb

This parallel circuit has three branches.

LED and resistor

Fan, driven by a motor

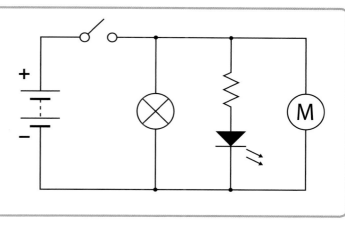

Circuit diagram for the circuit to the left

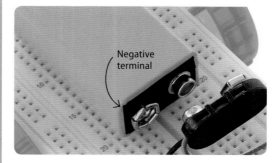

Negative terminal

What is "ground"?

Ground, or "earth", is the point of a circuit with the lowest voltage, and is often, but not always, zero volts (0v). In the circuits in a home, it is a metal spike in the ground, but in battery circuits, it is normally the negative terminal of the battery.

Breadboards

A breadboard is a plastic board with springy metal tracks inside that make it easy to connect up the wires and components in a circuit. Instead of needing to solder components and wires together, they can simply be pushed into the breadboard. This makes it easy to remove components if you have put them in the wrong place, and also means you can reuse components and the breadboard again and again.

How a breadboard works

Under the surface of a breadboard are rows and columns of metal tracks. These connect to metal springs that hold components and wires in place. The two columns on each side are joined together, and are useful for connecting the two terminals of a battery. The five holes in each row are connected. Therefore, any components or wires plugged into the same column on the side of the breadboard, or the same row in the body of the breadboard, are electrically connected.

The springy clips under the breadboard's surface allow components and wires to be plugged in, and hold them in place.

Positive battery wire

Negative battery wire

Anything plugged into this column will be connected to the battery's positive terminal.

The LED's positive leg is connected to the battery's positive terminal.

The two columns on either side of the breadboard are joined together along the length of the breadboard.

This leg of the resistor is connected to the battery's negative terminal.

The five holes in each row are connected, so the resistor's leg is connected to the LED's negative leg by the breadboard.

Different breadboards

There are several different kinds of breadboard. The most common are full-size breadboards, which have 64 rows. These are big enough for complex circuits, but mini breadboards are useful for smaller projects. Perforated boards are similiar to breadboards, but they require soldering, so they are used for more permanent circuits.

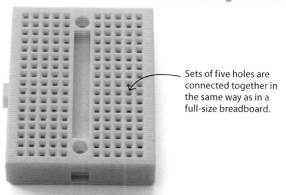

Sets of five holes are connected together in the same way as in a full-size breadboard.

Mini breadboards

These smaller versions do not have columns to carry power from the battery, but otherwise they work in just the same way as full-size boards. Most have clips along the sides, so they can be attached to each other. Some have holes for screws or adhesive backs, which enable you to mount the mini breadboard onto things.

Full-size breadboards

On a full-size breadboard, numbers and letters make it easy to follow circuit-building instructions – there is only one "C7" hole, for example. On full-size and mini breadboards, the gap along the middle is designed so that integrated circuits (ICs) can be plugged in. (For more on ICs, see p.17).

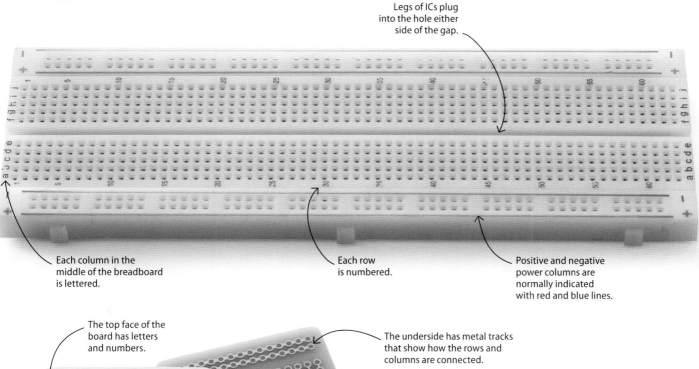

Legs of ICs plug into the hole either side of the gap.

Each column in the middle of the breadboard is lettered.

Each row is numbered.

Positive and negative power columns are normally indicated with red and blue lines.

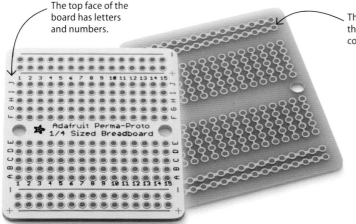

The top face of the board has letters and numbers.

The underside has metal tracks that show how the rows and columns are connected.

Perforated boards

The holes, or perforations, in a perforated board are joined together in rows and columns, just like in a breadboard. But wires and components cannot simply be plugged in – they have to be soldered into place.

Troubleshooting

Every project in this book includes an electric circuit. If you follow the instructions closely, and take care with each of the connections you make, your circuits should work in just the right way. But sometimes, things can go wrong. If they do, these troubleshooting pages should help you find and fix the problem.

Be safe

The projects in this book all have low-voltage power supplies – batteries or USB sockets – so there is almost no danger of you receiving an electric shock. However, it is best to disconnect the power supply when you are investigating what is wrong with your circuits. Also, don't try to use the skills you learn here to investigate other electric circuits, as they can be dangerous.

It may be a problem with the batteries...

The first thing to check is the power source. Make sure your batteries are connected in the right way, and that they have power. If there is heat – or even smoke – when you turn the circuit on, remove the batteries immediately. If the circuit is powered via USB, unplug the USB cable.

1 Make sure the batteries are inserted correctly. In a battery pack, the batteries' flat ends should be pressing against the springs.

2 Test that your batteries are working with a multimeter. Set your multimeter to "volts", and hold the red metal prong against the positive (+) battery terminal and the black metal prong against the negative (−) terminal. If the reading is zero or close to zero, the battery is flat and will need to be replaced.

It is normal for the meter to read a little lower than the marked voltage on the battery.

If you have an analog multimeter, set it to the next voltage range above the battery's voltage.

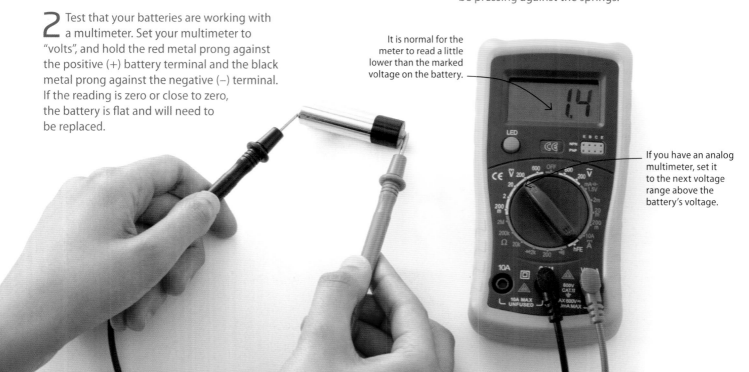

The circuit may be wired up incorrectly...

The circuits in this book have been carefully designed to allow electric current to move through the wires and components in just the right way to make things happen – such as lighting an LED or making a speaker produce sound. If just one wire or component is out of place, or one component has the wrong value, the circuit will not work.

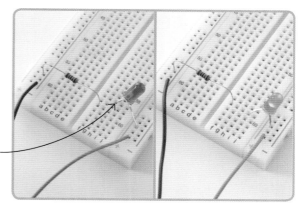

Here, the LED leg is sitting in row 57 of the breadboard, but it needs to be in row 59 to complete the circuit and light the LED.

1 If your circuit is on a breadboard, take particular care to make sure each wire or component's leg is in its correct place. Pay attention to the grid references given in the project description.

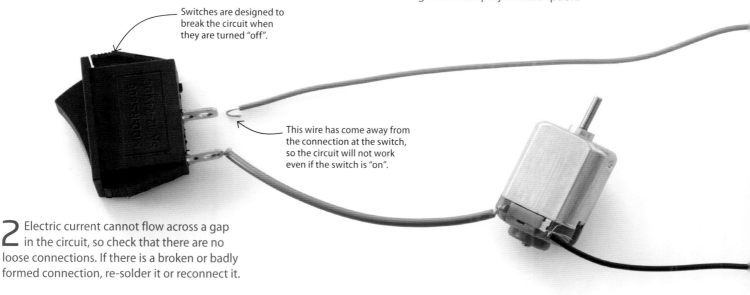

Switches are designed to break the circuit when they are turned "off".

This wire has come away from the connection at the switch, so the circuit will not work even if the switch is "on".

2 Electric current cannot flow across a gap in the circuit, so check that there are no loose connections. If there is a broken or badly formed connection, re-solder it or reconnect it.

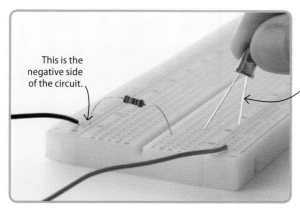

This is the negative side of the circuit.

The shorter leg of an LED is the negative side, so this LED should be turned around before being inserted into the breadboard.

3 Check that components such as LEDs, transistors, and electrolytic capacitors are connected the right way round. Each of these has a polarity, which means they have a (+) and a (–) side, which must be correctly connected to the circuit for them to work.

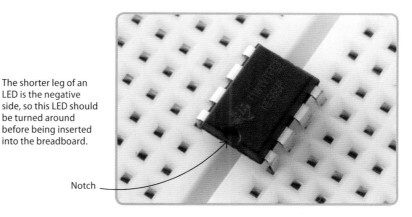

Notch

4 Integrated circuits (ICs) have equal numbers of legs either side. It is easy to put these into a circuit the wrong way round – you can check by making sure the semicircular "notch" at one end is in the same position as it is in the project steps.

It might be a short circuit...

A short circuit occurs when two metal parts – the stripped ends of wires or the legs of components, for example – are touching but shouldn't be. In a short circuit, electric current flows through a shortcut, missing out part of the circuit. The circuit will not work, and too much current will flow through one part of the circuit, which can damage components or cause the circuit to heat up.

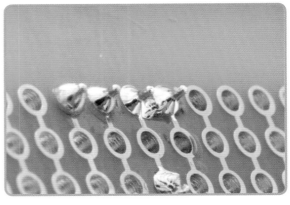

1 Solder becomes liquid when it is heated, and just like any liquid, it will cling together. When it solidifies, nearby blobs of solder may become joined and form a short circuit.

Some solder bridges can be very small, so you may need a magnifying glass to see them.

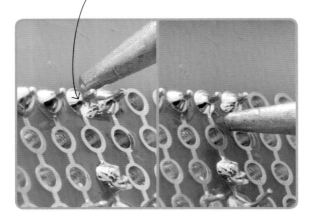

2 If you find a solder bridge, use a soldering iron to re-melt the solder and break the bridge, so the two connections are separate.

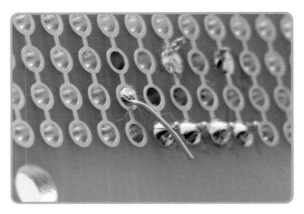

3 Short circuits also happen when the legs of two nearby components are touching but shouldn't be, so make sure you trim all legs.

It might be faulty components...

Sometimes a circuit doesn't work because one of the components in it is faulty. The most common faulty components are capacitors and resistors. You can use your multimeter to test each component in turn while they are still connected in the circuit – but turn off the circuit before you do this.

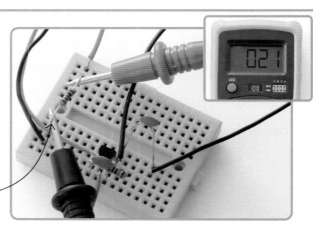

This resistor is 110 Ω, so we set our multimeter at 200.

1 To test a resistor, set your multimeter to the next resistance setting above what the resistor's value is (Reading a resistor, see p.15). Touch the metal prongs to each leg of the resistor. The meter should read very close to the value of the resistor, if it is not faulty.

2 To test a capacitor, unplug the power supply from the circuit and wait at least 30 seconds – this is to allow the capacitor to discharge the electrical energy it stores. Set your multimeter to the capacitance setting, and test the capacitor by touching the metal prongs to each leg. If the value is a lot higher or a lot lower than it should be, change the capacitor. If your multimeter doesn't have a capacitance setting, set the multimeter to the lowest resistance setting.

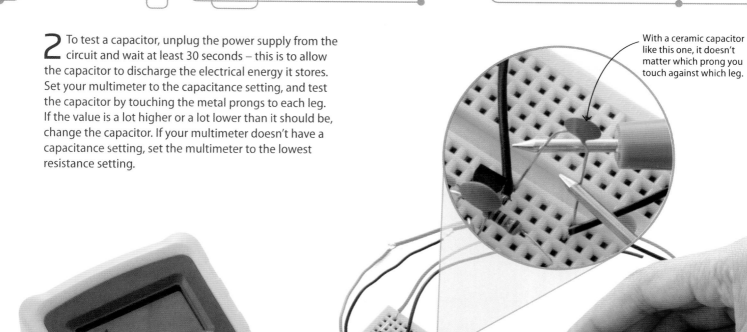

With a ceramic capacitor like this one, it doesn't matter which prong you touch against which leg.

The multimeter will send electrons from the black prong into the capacitor.

Hold the prongs steady for several seconds.

Electrolytic capacitors

Electrolytic capacitors have a polarity – electric current can only flow through them in one direction. When testing one of these kinds of capacitors, make sure you touch the negative metal prong to the negative leg, which is usually shorter and marked with a "–" on the capacitor's body.

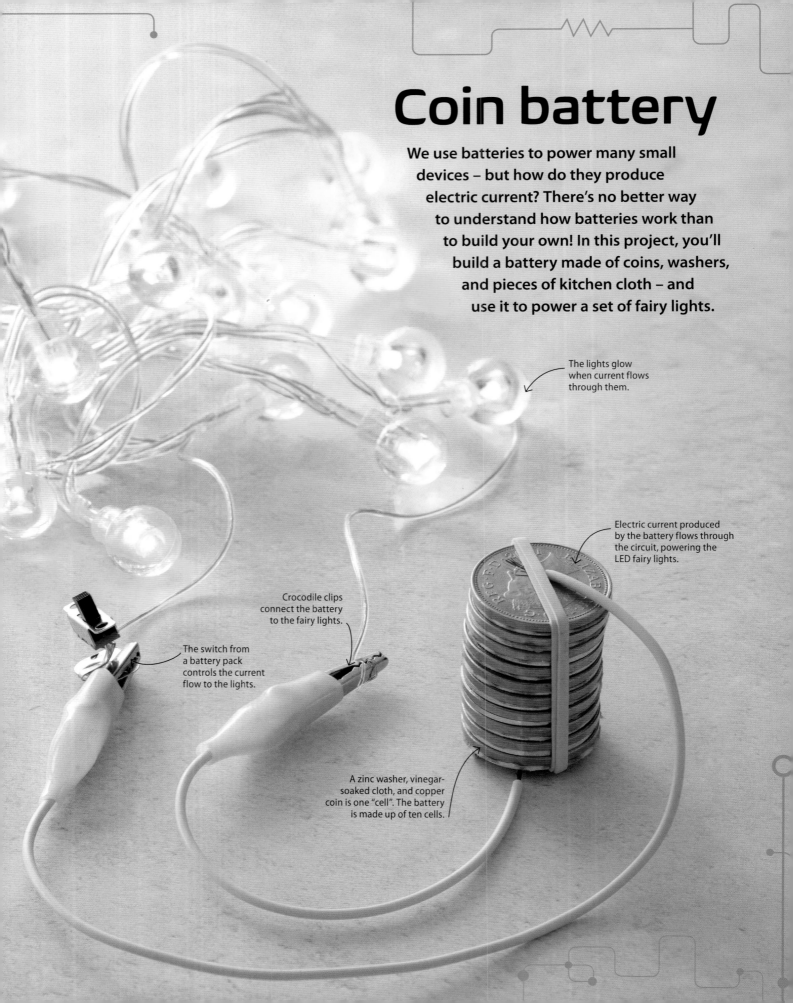

Coin battery

We use batteries to power many small devices – but how do they produce electric current? There's no better way to understand how batteries work than to build your own! In this project, you'll build a battery made of coins, washers, and pieces of kitchen cloth – and use it to power a set of fairy lights.

The lights glow when current flows through them.

Electric current produced by the battery flows through the circuit, powering the LED fairy lights.

Crocodile clips connect the battery to the fairy lights.

The switch from a battery pack controls the current flow to the lights.

A zinc washer, vinegar-soaked cloth, and copper coin is one "cell". The battery is made up of ten cells.

How to make a
Coin battery

To make this battery work well, you first need to make the coins sparkling clean – the solution you use to do this will also be part of the battery. Make sure you use galvanized washers: "galvanized" means "coated with zinc", and the metal zinc is a very important part of your battery.

Time
20 mins

Difficulty
Easy

What you need

From the toolbox:
- Pencil
- Scissors
- Multimeter

10x
Galvanized (zinc-coated) washers

1x
Rubber band

10x
"Copper" (copper-coated) coins

1x
Small dish of table salt

1x
3-volt fairy lights with a 2 x AA battery pack

1x
Small dish

Vinegar
30 ml (1 fl oz)

1x
Absorbent cloth

1x
Paper towel

1x
Spoon

1x
Wire with a crocodile clip at each end

When no more salt dissolves, the solution is saturated.

1 Pour about 30 ml (1 fl oz) of vinegar into the small dish. Keep adding salt and stirring until no more salt will dissolve.

The salt and vinegar clean the coins' surface layer.

2 Place the copper coins into the salt and vinegar solution. Leave them for about five minutes, until they turn shiny. Remove and dry them with a paper towel, then wash and dry your hands.

3 Using a coin as a template, cut out 10 circles from the absorbent cloth.

By folding the cloth, you can cut out more than one at a time.

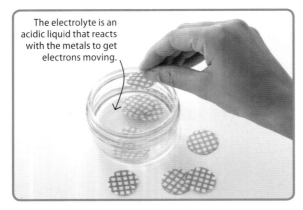

The electrolyte is an acidic liquid that reacts with the metals to get electrons moving.

4 Place the discs of kitchen cloth into the dish of salt and vinegar solution, and leave them to soak for a few minutes. The vinegar will be the electrolyte in your battery.

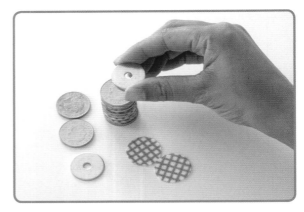

5 Lay down a galvanized washer, stack a cloth disc on top, and then a copper coin on top of that. Repeat in this order until all the materials are in a neat pile, making sure that the top disc is a coin.

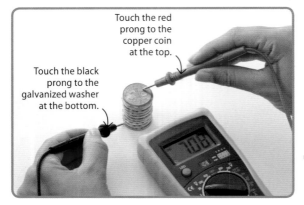

Touch the red prong to the copper coin at the top.

Touch the black prong to the galvanized washer at the bottom.

Using a multimeter see pp.28–29

6 Set the multimeter to read voltage, in the range between 1 and 10 volts. Touch the prongs to the top and bottom of the stack. The voltage should read between 6 and 8 volts.

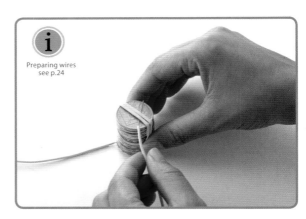

Preparing wires see p.24

7 Cut the crocodile-clip wire in half, and strip the freshly cut ends of the two wires. Fix each wire to the top and bottom of the battery. Secure the wires in place by wrapping the rubber band around the pile.

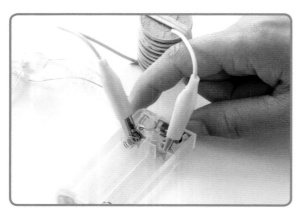

8 Clip the crocodile clips to the metal connections inside the battery pack: the wire from the washer should be attached to the springy connection.

9 Flip the switch on the battery pack, and the fairy lights should illuminate.

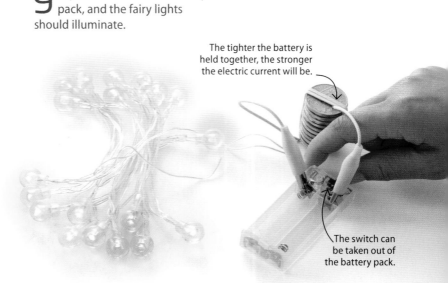

The tighter the battery is held together, the stronger the electric current will be.

The switch can be taken out of the battery pack.

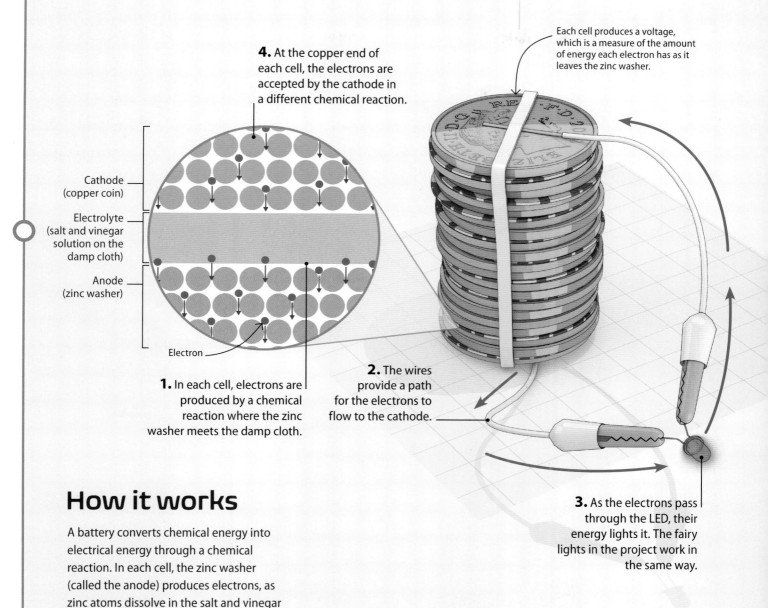

4. At the copper end of each cell, the electrons are accepted by the cathode in a different chemical reaction.

Each cell produces a voltage, which is a measure of the amount of energy each electron has as it leaves the zinc washer.

Cathode (copper coin)

Electrolyte (salt and vinegar solution on the damp cloth)

Anode (zinc washer)

Electron

1. In each cell, electrons are produced by a chemical reaction where the zinc washer meets the damp cloth.

2. The wires provide a path for the electrons to flow to the cathode.

3. As the electrons pass through the LED, their energy lights it. The fairy lights in the project work in the same way.

How it works

A battery converts chemical energy into electrical energy through a chemical reaction. In each cell, the zinc washer (called the anode) produces electrons, as zinc atoms dissolve in the salt and vinegar solution (the electrolyte). Electrons flow through the wires, and are taken in at the copper end (the cathode), where they take part in another chemical reaction in the electrolyte. The voltages of all of the cells add up, giving the electrons that leave the battery at the bottom enough energy to light the LEDs.

Real-world inventions
The first battery

Italian scientist Alessandro Volta invented the battery in 1799. Just like the battery you have built, it was made with copper and zinc discs. Volta used cloth discs soaked in brine (salty water), rather than discs of kitchen cloth soaked in salt and vinegar.

Motor

Electric motors convert electrical energy into kinetic (movement) energy. In this project, you'll build a simple motor using electric current supplied by a battery. The current flows through a coil, producing a magnetic field that interacts with the magnetic field of a permanent magnet. The magnetic forces between the coil and the magnet make the coil spin at high speed.

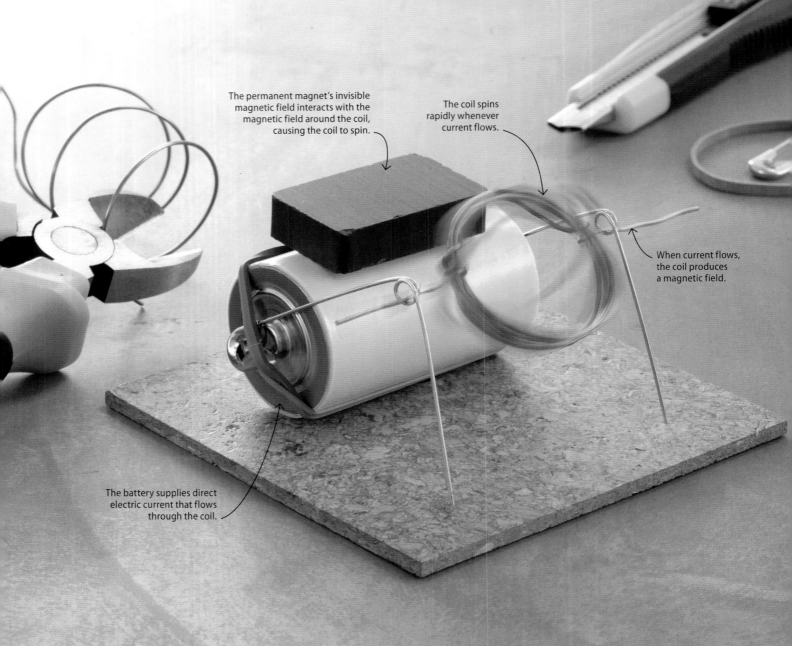

The permanent magnet's invisible magnetic field interacts with the magnetic field around the coil, causing the coil to spin.

The coil spins rapidly whenever current flows.

When current flows, the coil produces a magnetic field.

The battery supplies direct electric current that flows through the coil.

How to make a
Motor

The part of your motor that turns (the rotor) is a coil made of copper wire. The wire has a coating that prevents electricity from passing through the circuit, so it is important to scrape the ends of the wire so an electrical connection can be made.

Time	Be aware	Difficulty
15 mins	Requires utility knife use. The motor can get hot if left to run.	Easy

What you need

From the toolbox:
- Utility knife
- Wire cutters
- Ruler

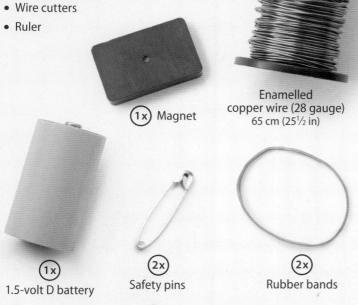

1x Magnet

Enamelled copper wire (28 gauge) 65 cm (25½ in)

1x 1.5-volt D battery

2x Safety pins

2x Rubber bands

1x Base 10 x 10 cm (4 x 4 in)

This is a cork tile, but anything that the pins can be stuck into can be used for the base.

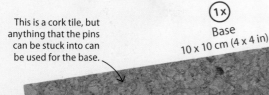

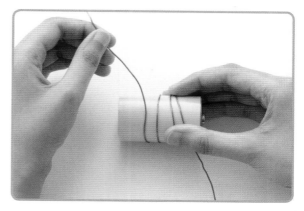

1 Make five turns of the enamelled copper wire around the battery. Leave about 5 cm (2 in) of wire on each end.

The two ends should stick out from each side of the coil.

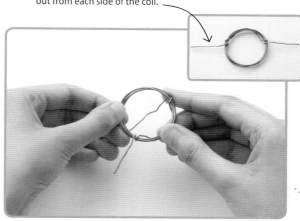

2 Take the wire off the battery. Flatten it into a circle, then wrap the two ends around the coil at opposite sides of the circle to hold the coil together.

3 Using the utility knife, scrape off the enamel coating on the free ends of the wire, right up to the coil, so that the shiny copper is exposed.

Utility knife see p.20

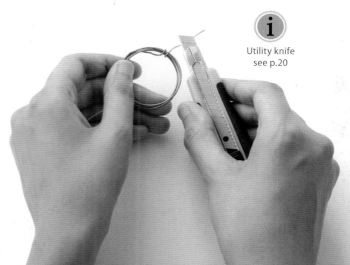

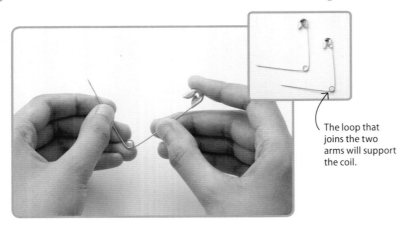

The loop that joins the two arms will support the coil.

4 Bend open both safety pins so that the arms on each form a 90-degree angle. Take care with the sharp points.

5 Wrap the rubber band around the battery. It needs to be tight, so double it up if necessary to increase the tension.

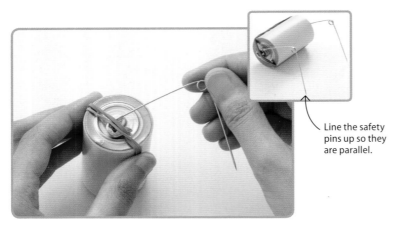

Line the safety pins up so they are parallel.

6 Push the clasps of the safety pins underneath the rubber band, one at each end of the battery, so that they are held firmly against the battery's terminals.

7 Place the construction onto the base. Push the sharp points into the cork, making sure the loops are at the same height.

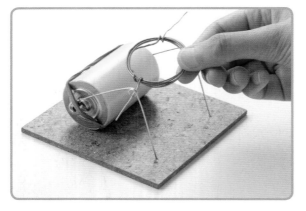

8 Gently feed the ends of the copper wire through the loops in the safety pins, so that the coil is suspended. Straighten the pins again afterwards.

9 Place the magnet on top of the battery. It will stay there without any glue because the battery case is made of steel, a magnetic material.

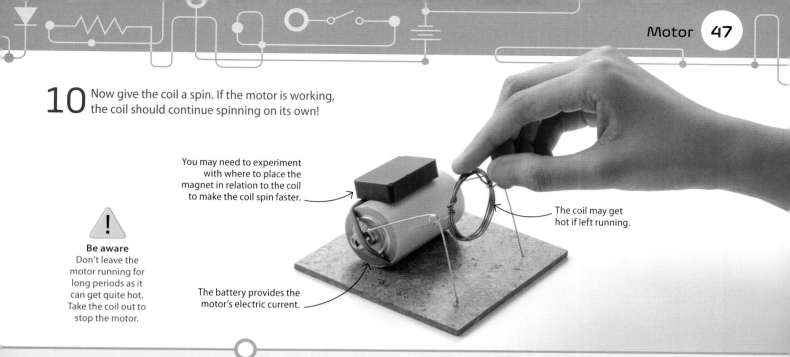

10 Now give the coil a spin. If the motor is working, the coil should continue spinning on its own!

You may need to experiment with where to place the magnet in relation to the coil to make the coil spin faster.

The coil may get hot if left running.

⚠️ **Be aware**
Don't leave the motor running for long periods as it can get quite hot. Take the coil out to stop the motor.

The battery provides the motor's electric current.

How it works

Electricity and magnetism are closely linked, and when electricity flows through the coil, it creates a magnetic field around it.

1. The permanent magnet and the magnetized coil each have a north and a south pole. Like poles (north and north or south and south) repel, while opposite poles attract.

North (red) pole.

Coil

South (blue) pole.

2. When you spin the coil, its south magnetic pole is attracted to the north pole of the magnet. The spin's momentum takes the coil's south magnetic pole beyond the north magnetic pole of the magnet.

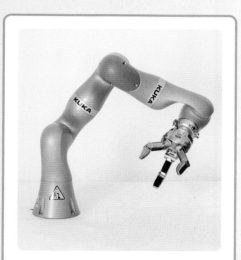

Real-world inventions
Robot arm

Motors are used in many tools and machines, including cordless drills, small toys, and even robot arms. The fine precision needed by a robot is achieved by motors located in each joint of the arm.

3. The north pole of the coil is then repelled by the north magnetic pole of the magnet. This process increases in momentum, which keeps the motor turning.

The coil's spin is affected by the coil's size, the material it is made of, and the amount of current flowing through it.

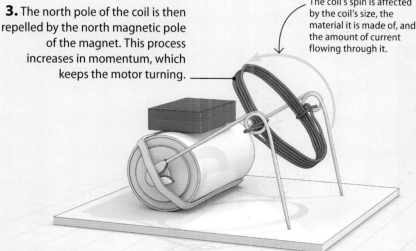

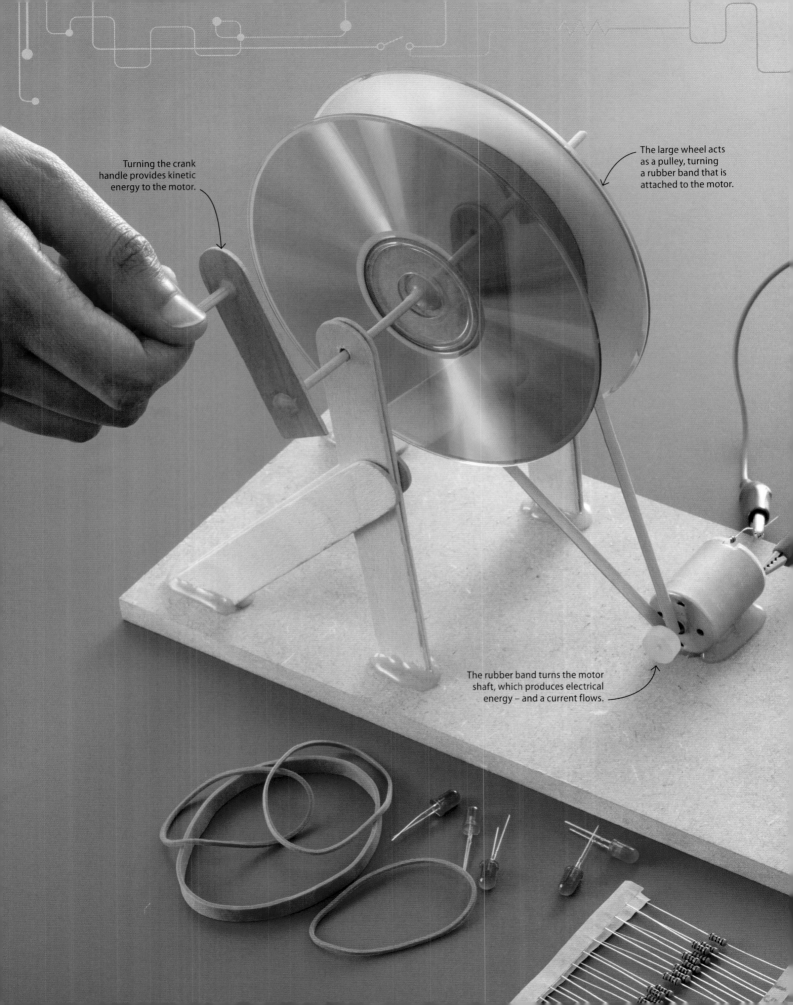

Turning the crank handle provides kinetic energy to the motor.

The large wheel acts as a pulley, turning a rubber band that is attached to the motor.

The rubber band turns the motor shaft, which produces electrical energy – and a current flows.

Generator

Most of the electricity supplied to homes is produced by machines called generators, which convert kinetic (movement) energy into electrical energy. A generator contains coils of wire arranged around a spinning shaft, surrounded by magnets – just like a motor. In fact, you can use a motor to generate electricity – and that's just what you'll be doing in this activity.

The LED lights up when a current flows.

How to make a
Generator

Make sure you follow the instructions carefully as this build relies on the supporting frame being sturdy. Try to find a medium-sized rubber band – if it is too big or too small, it will not drive the motor shaft around effectively. It's okay if you can't find any old CDs – try to find something sturdy with the same dimensions of 12 cm (4¾ in) in diameter.

Time	Be aware	Difficulty
45 mins	Requires hot-glue gun, hacksaw, drill, utility knife, and wire cutter use.	Medium

What you need

From the toolbox:

- Utility knife
- Cutting mat
- Hot-glue gun
- Adhesive putty
- Ruler
- Scrap wood and clamps
- Hacksaw
- Drill
- 3 mm (⅛ in) drill bit for wood
- Wire cutters

(1x) Green LED

(2x) Wires with crocodile clips at each end

(1x) Rubber band

(1x) 150 kΩ resistor

(1x) 6–9-volt motor

(2x) Compact discs (CDs)

(1x) Corrugated cardboard

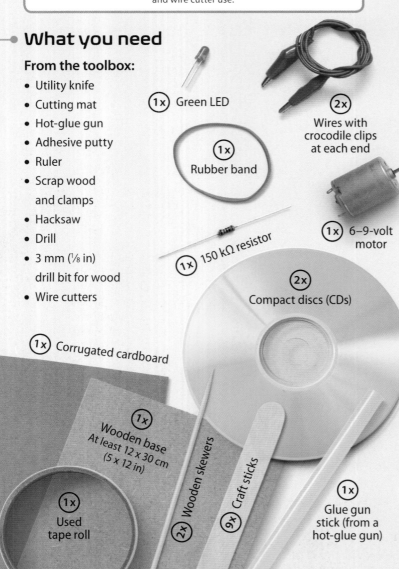

(1x) Wooden base At least 12 x 30 cm (5 x 12 in)

(1x) Used tape roll

(2x) Wooden skewers

(9x) Craft sticks

(1x) Glue gun stick (from a hot-glue gun)

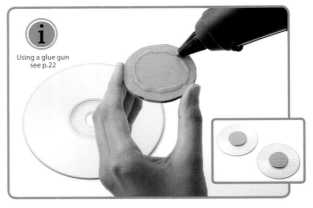

Using a glue gun see p.22

1 Cut out two cardboard discs, with diameters smaller than the inside diameter of the tape roll. Using the hot-glue gun, stick the discs over the holes in the centres of the CDs.

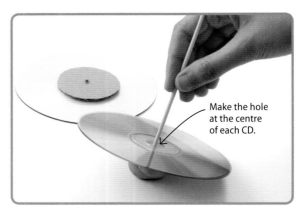

Make the hole at the centre of each CD.

2 Use a wooden skewer to poke a hole through the centre of each cardboard disc. A lump of adhesive putty will help you make a clean hole.

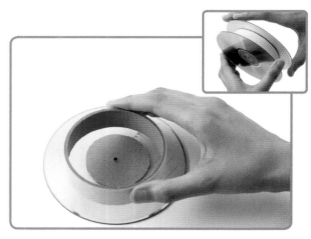

3 Run glue around the edges of the empty tape roll. Press the roll onto one of the CDs, over the cardboard disc, making sure it is centred. Next, press the other CD onto the tape roll, with the cardboard disc facing inwards.

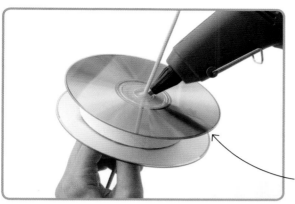

The main pulley wheel is complete.

4 Once the glue has dried, push the skewer through the centres of the cardboard discs to form the shaft. Make sure there is an equal length of skewer on each side, then glue the shaft to the cardboard on each side.

Clamping the sticks to a scrap piece of wood will help to hold them in place.

Hacksaw
see p.21

5 Using a hacksaw, cut 1 cm (⅜ in) off one end of four craft sticks. Next, cut one end off four more craft sticks at a 45° angle, starting 2 cm (¾ in) up one side.

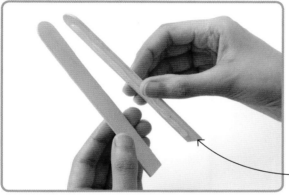

Make sure the sticks are aligned.

6 Glue together two of the straight-cut craft sticks, and then repeat with the other two. These are the legs that will support the generator's pulley wheel.

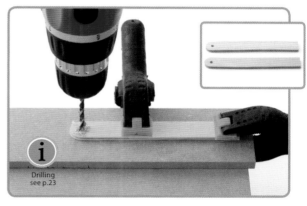

Drilling
see p.23

7 Using a drill bit slightly wider than the wooden skewer, drill a hole through the middle of each of the legs, about 1 cm (⅜ in) from the rounded end.

8 Using a utility knife, cut two discs, each about 6 mm (¼ in) thick, from an unused glue gun stick.

! Hold the glue firmly so it doesn't roll as you are cutting it.

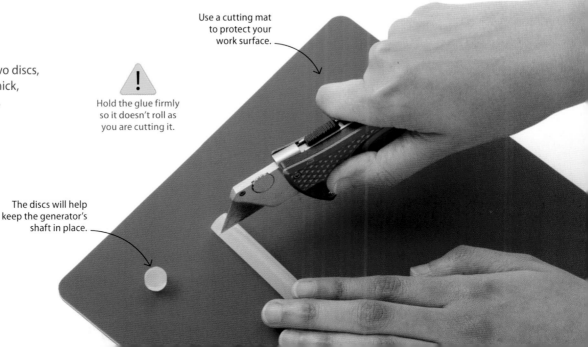

Use a cutting mat to protect your work surface.

The discs will help keep the generator's shaft in place.

9 Stretch the rubber band around the tape roll. This will be the belt of the pulley system that attaches to the motor and turns the generator.

10 Using the pointed end of a skewer, make a hole in the centre of each glue stick disc. Push one of the discs onto one side of the shaft of the pulley wheel. Set aside the second glue disc.

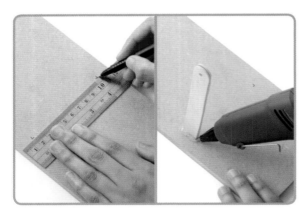

11 On the wooden base, make a mark about 2 cm (¾ in) in from each side, about 12 cm (5 in) from one end. Glue one of the legs on top of one of the marks, and wait for the glue to dry.

Make sure the shaft can turn freely.

12 Push one end of the shaft through the hole in the leg already in place, and feed the other end through the hole in the other leg. Glue the second leg on top of the second mark.

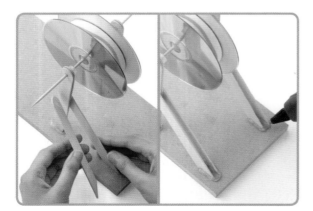

13 Use the angle-cut craft sticks to make supports for the legs. Glue the rounded ends to the legs, one on each side of each leg, and the flat angled ends to the base.

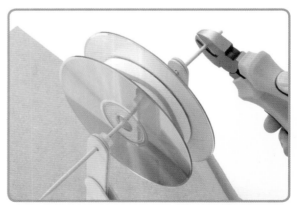

14 Use the wire cutters to carefully trim the ends of the pulley shaft on both sides, leaving about 4 cm (1½ in) on each side of the legs.

15 Using the last craft stick, cut a length of about 6 cm (2⅜ in) from it for the generator's crank handle. Drill a hole about 1 cm (⅜ in) in from each end.

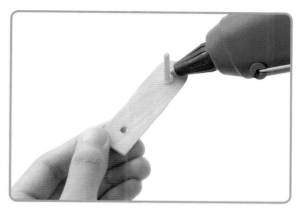

16 Cut a piece of wooden skewer about 2½ cm (1 in) long and glue it into the hole at the rounded end of the handle.

17 Push the second glue disc (see step 8) onto the end of the pulley shaft – at the same end as the first glue disc.

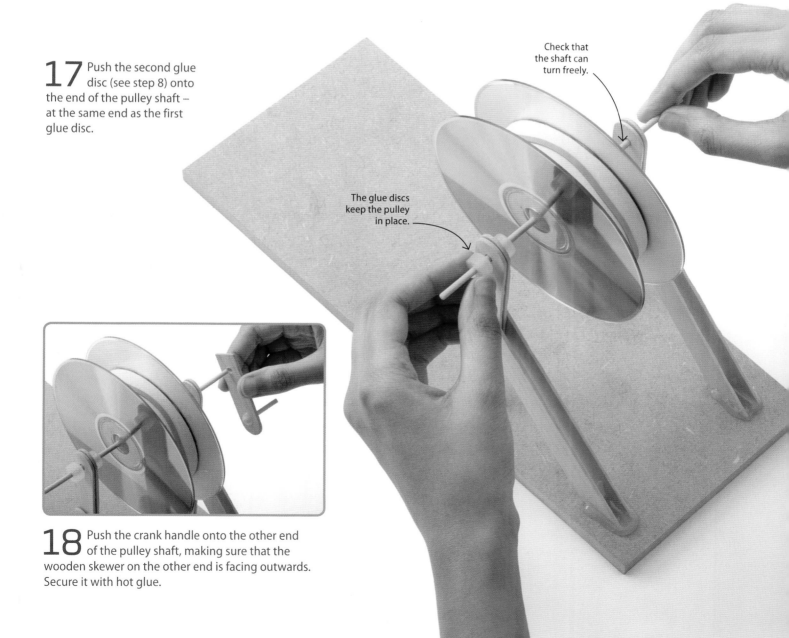

Check that the shaft can turn freely.

The glue discs keep the pulley in place.

18 Push the crank handle onto the other end of the pulley shaft, making sure that the wooden skewer on the other end is facing outwards. Secure it with hot glue.

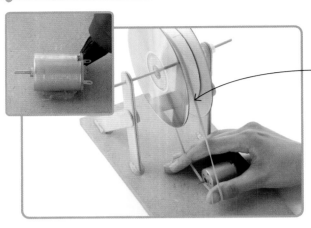

Make sure that the centre of the pulley is in line with the motor's shaft.

19 Find a place for the motor in the centre of the base, far enough from the pulley that the rubber band is taut. Glue the motor down and then stretch the rubber band over the motor's shaft.

20 Cut another 6 mm (¼ in) thick disc from the glue gun stick. Push the point of a skewer into its centre, but do not push all the way through. Push the glue stick disc onto the shaft of the motor.

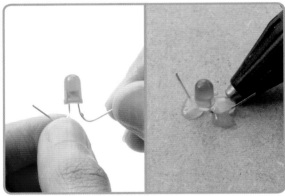

21 Carefully bend the legs of the LED up. Next, glue it to the base with a blob of hot glue.

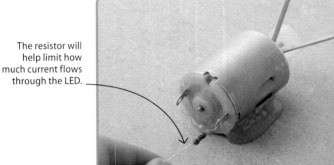

The resistor will help limit how much current flows through the LED.

22 Attach one end of the 150 kΩ resistor to one of the terminals of the motor. It doesn't matter which one.

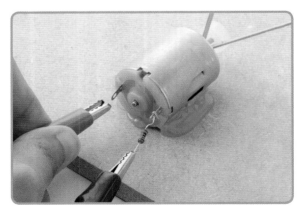

23 Using the crocodile wires, connect the clip of one of the wires to the free end of the resistor, and the clip of the other wire to the other terminal of the motor.

24 Connect the other ends of the two wires to the two legs of the LED. The generator is ready to operate.

25 Turn the handle of the generator. Make sure the shaft of the motor is turning. LEDs only light up when the current flows in one direction, so if it doesn't light up, it may mean that the current is flowing the wrong way. Try turning the handle the other way, or switching the crocodile clips attached to the LED, as this will switch the direction of current from the motor.

Turning the handle spins the pulley. This spin is transferred to the motor via the rubber band.

As the motor spins, it creates an electric current in the circuit, and the LED lights up.

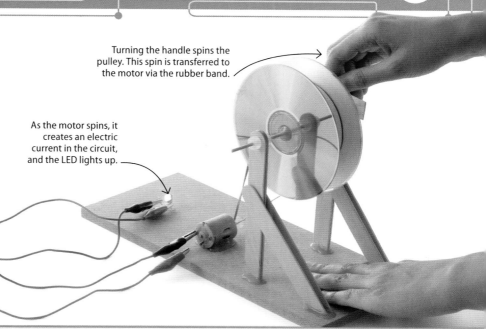

How it works

A motor is designed so that its shaft spins when electric current flows through it. However, this process can be reversed: spinning the motor's shaft can be used to produce an electric current. Inside the motor are static magnets as well as three coils of wire that can spin.

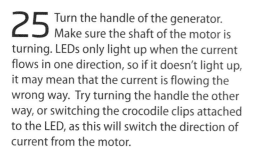

Real-world inventions
Hydroelectric power

Nearly one-fifth of the world's electricity is generated by hydroelectricity (the energy of moving water). The machines in this picture are turbines at the Hoover Dam in the US. The turbines spin as water pushes through them, turning generators that supply electricity.

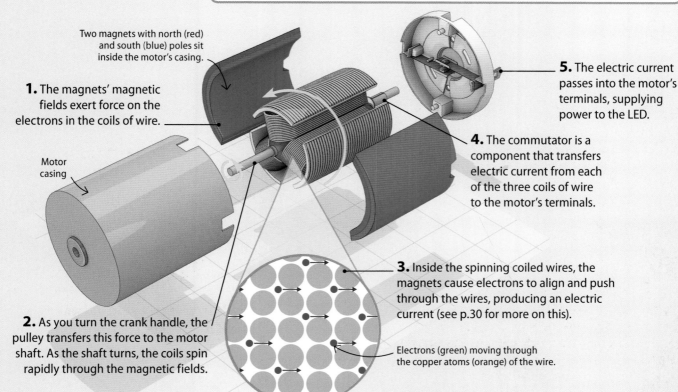

Two magnets with north (red) and south (blue) poles sit inside the motor's casing.

1. The magnets' magnetic fields exert force on the electrons in the coils of wire.

Motor casing

5. The electric current passes into the motor's terminals, supplying power to the LED.

4. The commutator is a component that transfers electric current from each of the three coils of wire to the motor's terminals.

3. Inside the spinning coiled wires, the magnets cause electrons to align and push through the wires, producing an electric current (see p.30 for more on this).

2. As you turn the crank handle, the pulley transfers this force to the motor shaft. As the shaft turns, the coils spin rapidly through the magnetic fields.

Electrons (green) moving through the copper atoms (orange) of the wire.

The propellers spin as electric current from the batteries passes through two motors mounted on the top of the fan.

Handheld fan

Keep cool with this useful handheld fan! In this project, you'll be using batteries to power two motors with propellers attached, to produce a cooling breeze. You will be wiring the motors in parallel, which means that each of the motors is on a separate branch of the circuit, so that each one receives the full voltage the batteries provide.

How to make a
Handheld fan

For this project, you will need to get hold of a battery pack with a built-in switch. You will also need to find pieces of plastic or wood to act as a platform for the motors. They need to be wide enough to hold the motors, and long enough that the propeller blades won't touch once they are installed.

Time	Be aware	Difficulty
30 mins	Requires hot-glue gun and soldering iron use.	Easy

What you need

From the toolbox

- Hot-glue gun
- Wire strippers
- Soldering iron and solder

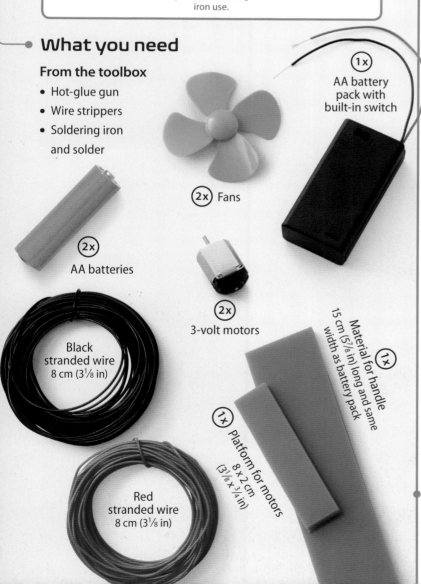

2x AA batteries

2x Fans

1x AA battery pack with built-in switch

2x 3-volt motors

1x Material for handle 15 cm (5⅞ in) long and same width as battery pack

1x Platform for motors 8 x 2 cm (3⅛ x ¾ in)

Black stranded wire 8 cm (3⅛ in)

Red stranded wire 8 cm (3⅛ in)

Using a glue gun see p.22

1 Glue the motor platform to the top of the battery pack, making sure it is in the centre. Make sure that you can still open the battery pack.

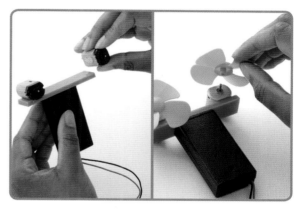

2 Glue one motor onto each end of the platform, with the shafts pointing away from the side of the battery pack with the switch, and the motor terminals facing down. Next, slide on the propellers.

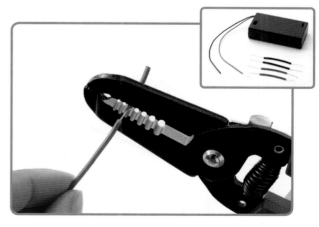

3 Cut and strip two black wires and two red wires, each about 4 cm (1½ in) long, and strip the battery pack wires.

4 Twist the stripped ends of the red wires onto the left terminals of each motor.

5 Twist the stripped ends of the black wires on the right terminals of each motor.

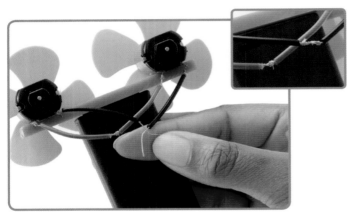

6 Twist the ends of the red wires together, and the ends of the black wires together.

You can shorten the battery pack wires if they get in the way.

7 Twist the end of the red battery wire around the twisted black wires. Then twist the end of the black battery wire around the twisted red wires.

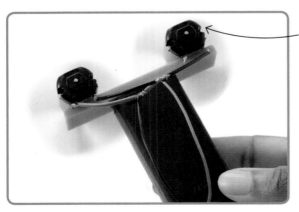

The direction the fans rotate in is determined by the polarity of the motors, which you can find out by testing them.

8 Flip the switch on the battery pack to test whether the propellers create a forward-blowing breeze. If the air is blowing backwards, switch the black and red battery pack wires around.

Soldering see pp.25–26

9 Once you are happy with the flow of air, solder all of the wire connections.

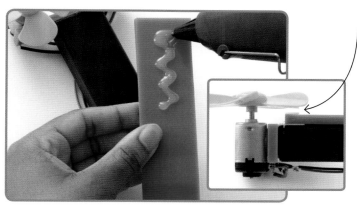

Make sure the fans are clear of the handle when they spin and that you can still open the battery pack.

10 Glue a handle to the front of the battery pack that is the same width as it.

11 Your fan is now finished. When you turn it on, it will create a refreshing breeze.

How it works

When you wire circuit components in parallel, each component receives the same voltage, so in your handheld fan, each motor receives the full 3 volts from the battery pack. Two motors in parallel will use twice the power, however, so the batteries will run down more quickly.

2. Each motor receives all the energy of the electrons that pass through it.

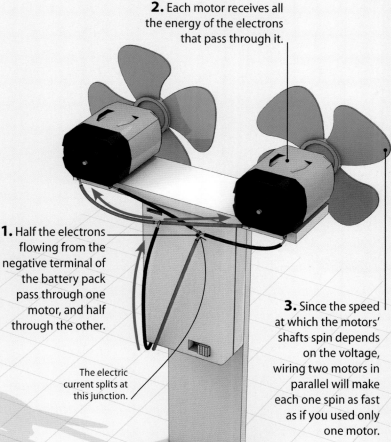

1. Half the electrons flowing from the negative terminal of the battery pack pass through one motor, and half through the other.

The electric current splits at this junction.

3. Since the speed at which the motors' shafts spin depends on the voltage, wiring two motors in parallel will make each one spin as fast as if you used only one motor.

Real-world inventions
Car headlights

Car headlights are wired in parallel. If they were wired in series, then if one lamp stopped working, the other one would also not work, and both would gradually get dimmer as the battery drains.

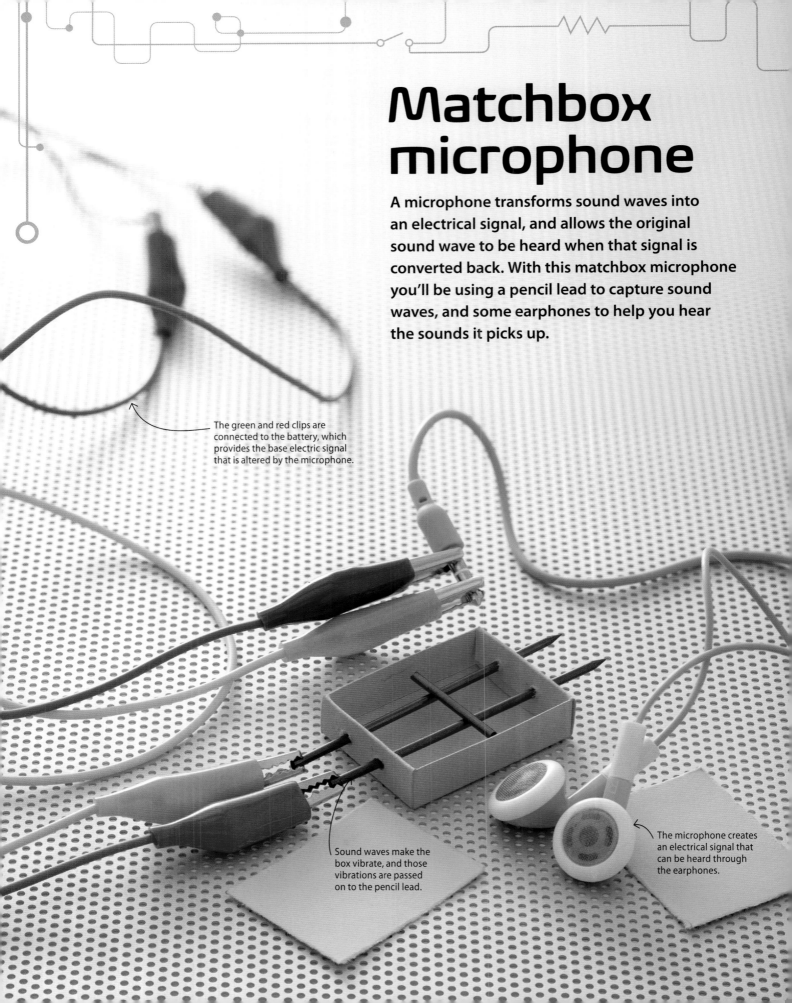

Matchbox microphone

A microphone transforms sound waves into an electrical signal, and allows the original sound wave to be heard when that signal is converted back. With this matchbox microphone you'll be using a pencil lead to capture sound waves, and some earphones to help you hear the sounds it picks up.

The green and red clips are connected to the battery, which provides the base electric signal that is altered by the microphone.

Sound waves make the box vibrate, and those vibrations are passed on to the pencil lead.

The microphone creates an electrical signal that can be heard through the earphones.

How to make a
Matchbox microphone

The safest and easiest way to get the pencil leads you need is to buy mechanical pencil lead refills. Also, it is best to use old or cheap earphones, in case they get damaged.

Time
15 mins

Be aware
Requires bradawl and utility knife use.

Difficulty
Easy

What you need

From the toolbox
- Utility knife
- Bradawl

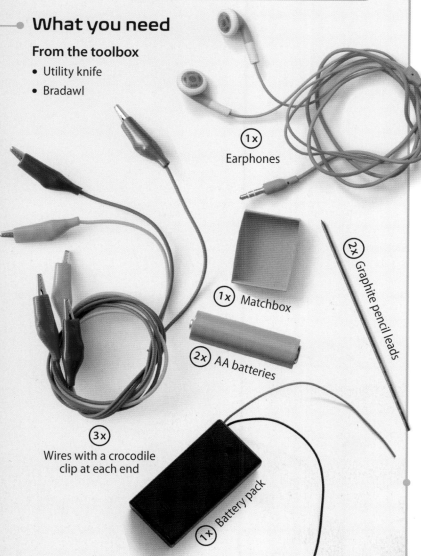

(1x) Earphones

(1x) Matchbox

(2x) AA batteries

(2x) Graphite pencil leads

(3x) Wires with a crocodile clip at each end

(1x) Battery pack

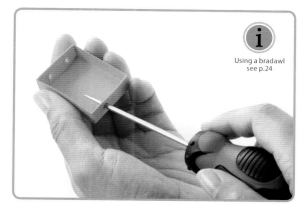

Using a bradawl see p.24

1 Use the bradawl to pierce two holes about 1 cm (⅜ in) apart in one end of the box, then repeat for the other end. Be careful not to hurt your hand when making the piercing.

Utility knife see p.20

2 Gently scratch one side of both pencil leads with the sharp edge of the utility knife to create a flat side on each.

3 Push the pencil leads through the holes in the box, as shown. Let the pencil leads stick out from each end of the box. Twist them around so the flat side faces up.

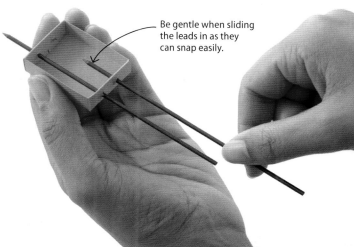

Be gentle when sliding the leads in as they can snap easily.

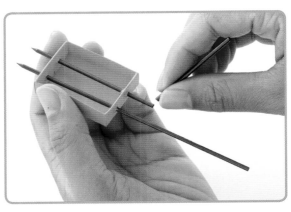

4 Snap the ends of the pencil leads, so that about 1 cm (³⁄₈ in) remains sticking out from the box.

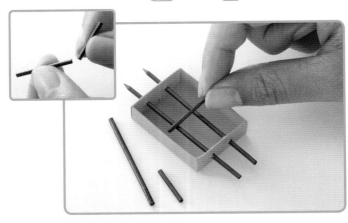

5 Snap a piece of pencil lead that's slightly shorter than the width of the box from one of the leftover pieces. Place it flat-side down across the other two leads, to bridge the gap between them.

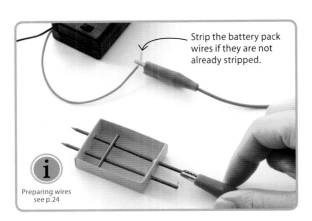

Strip the battery pack wires if they are not already stripped.

ⓘ
Preparing wires
see p.24

6 Using one of the crocodile clip wires, connect one of the pencil leads to one of the battery pack wires.

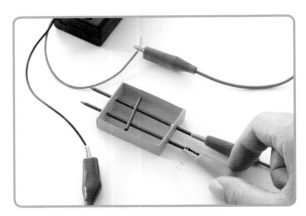

7 Use a different crocodile clip wire to connect to the remaining battery pack wire. Finally, take a third crocodile clip wire and connect it to the remaining pencil lead.

8 You should have two crocodile clips that are left free. Connect one crocodile clip to the tip of the metal part of the earphone jack, and the other one to the other end of the metal part.

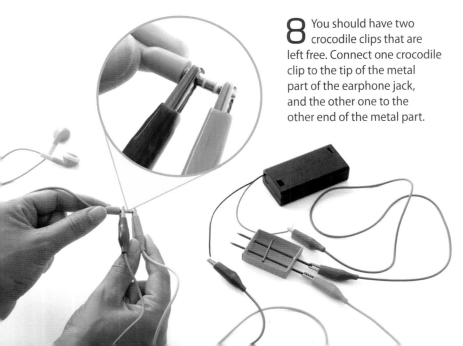

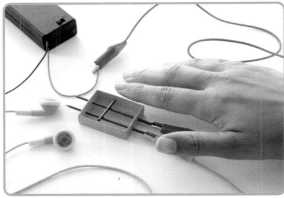

9 Insert the earphones into your ears, switch on the battery pack if it has a switch, and then gently tap the box. You should hear the tapping sound through one of the earphones. Next, try speaking into the box!

How it works

Pencil "leads" are not made of lead: they are made of a material called graphite mixed with clay. Graphite conducts electricity, but not very well: it has a high resistance to electric current.

Real-world inventions
Audio signal

The varying electric current microphones produce is called an audio signal. It is a copy of the changes in air pressure of a sound wave. The audio signal can be recorded digitally inside a computer, and then displayed on, and manipulated by, a computer.

No sound

1. When you connect the circuit, an electric current flows from the battery, through the graphite and earphones, and back to the battery.

2. The bridging lead makes a good connection with the other two leads when the microphone is picking up no sound, allowing the current to flow.

3. Any sounds directed at the box cause the bridging lead to jump up and down, disturbing the flow of electric current through the circuit.

Sound

4. When the contact is worse, less current flows, and when the contact is better, more current flows. The variation in the electric current matches the pattern of vibration caused by the sound waves.

5. The varying current causes the tiny speakers in the earphones to move to and fro, recreating the original sound waves.

Bugbot

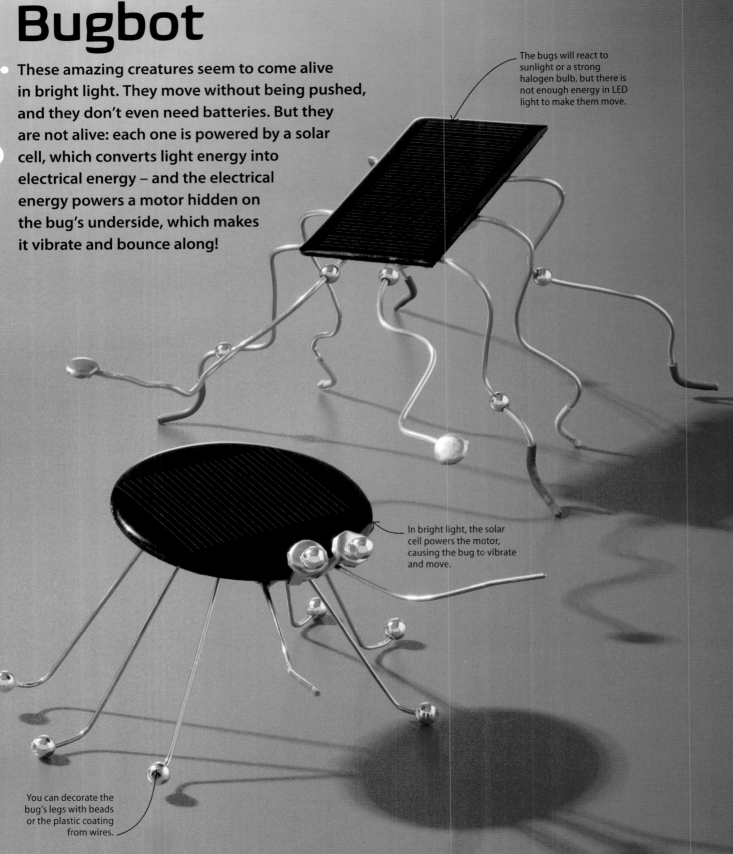

These amazing creatures seem to come alive in bright light. They move without being pushed, and they don't even need batteries. But they are not alive: each one is powered by a solar cell, which converts light energy into electrical energy – and the electrical energy powers a motor hidden on the bug's underside, which makes it vibrate and bounce along!

The bugs will react to sunlight or a strong halogen bulb, but there is not enough energy in LED light to make them move.

In bright light, the solar cell powers the motor, causing the bug to vibrate and move.

You can decorate the bug's legs with beads or the plastic coating from wires.

How to make a
Bugbot

For this project, you need a solar cell and a vibrating motor. There are various kinds of these motors – look for a "coin" or "pancake" one, and make sure it has two leads, not three. Avoid any labelled a "linear resonant activator" as they will not work in this build.

Time	Be aware	Difficulty
15 mins	Requires soldering and hot-glue gun use	Easy

What you need

From the toolbox

- Wire cutters
- Soldering iron and solder
- Pliers
- Hot-glue gun

3x Large paper clips

2x Small paper clips

1x Mini 3-volt solar cell

1x 3-volt "coin" or "pancake" vibration motor

2x Small silver beads

1x Red stranded wire 4 cm (1½ in)

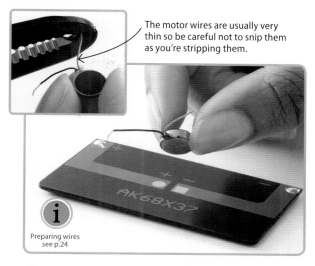

The motor wires are usually very thin so be careful not to snip them as you're stripping them.

ⓘ Preparing wires see p.24

1 Strip the motor's wires. If your motor has a self-adhesive pad, use it to stick the motor to the middle of the solar cell's underside – otherwise use a little hot glue.

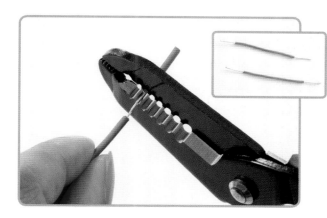

2 If your motor's wires can reach the solar panel's terminals, skip this step. If not, cut and strip two short stranded wires just long enough to reach from the ends of the motor wires to the terminals of the solar cell, to bridge the gap.

3 Use the short wires and solder to connect each motor wire to a terminal of the solar cell – it doesn't matter which one goes where. If your solar cell has long wires, just solder those to the motor wires.

ⓘ Soldering see pp.25–26

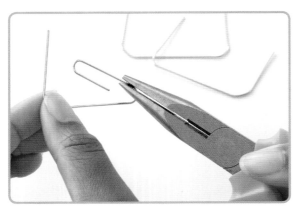

4 Using the pliers, unfold three paper clips, then trim the ends and bend them into wide "U" shapes, so each one looks like a pair of insect legs.

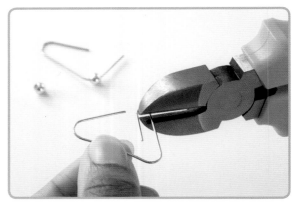

Using a glue gun see p.22

5 Use hot glue to attach each pair of legs to the underside of the solar cell. Make sure the legs don't touch the exposed parts of the wires, to avoid causing a short circuit.

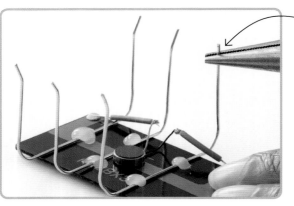

Use the pliers to bend the ends of the wire to create little feet.

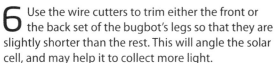

6 Use the wire cutters to trim either the front or the back set of the bugbot's legs so that they are slightly shorter than the rest. This will angle the solar cell, and may help it to collect more light.

7 If you like, you can make eyes and antennae using smaller paper clips and beads. But don't add too many things, or your bugbot will become too heavy for the motor to move.

Your bugbot will need to be exposed to plenty of bright light to work.

8 To make it move, take your bugbot outside if it is very sunny, or place it underneath a halogen lamp. It will work best on a smooth, flat surface.

The vibrating bug will glide across the surface.

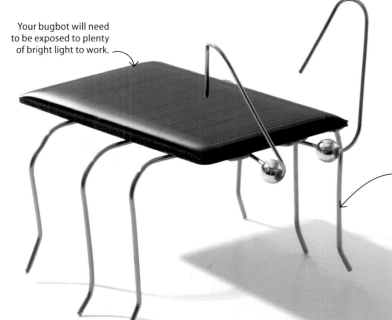

How it works

The bugbot is a simple circuit – the solar panel provides electrons that are used to power the vibration motor, which makes the bugbot move.

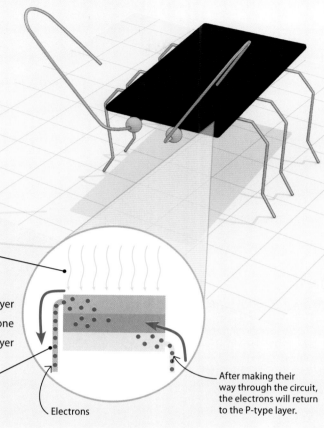

1. The solar panel is made up of two layers – the N-type and the P-type, which are separated by a barrier called the depletion zone. When bright light shines on the solar panel, electrons are dislodged from their atoms in the depletion zone.

N-type layer
Depletion zone
P-type layer

After making their way through the circuit, the electrons will return to the P-type layer.

Electrons

2. The electrons are pushed up through the N-type layer, and into the circuit. This is the electric current that powers the bugbot.

Real-world inventions
Smartphone

There is a vibration motor inside every smartphone. In most smartphones, it is the only moving part. When a call comes in, the motor activates, whirring round and making the whole phone vibrate. This is particularly useful when the phone's ringer is turned to silent.

3. Inside the motor is an unevenly distributed weight. When electrons flow into the motor, the uneven weight spins. Its unevenness causes the motor to vibrate.

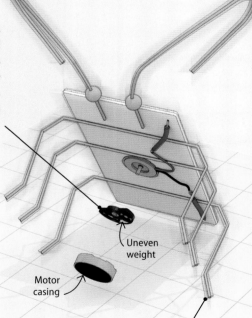

Uneven weight

Motor casing

4. The vibration makes the whole bugbot shake, and as it does so, it lifts off the surface and lands again many times each second, so the bugbot bounces along the surface in tiny hops.

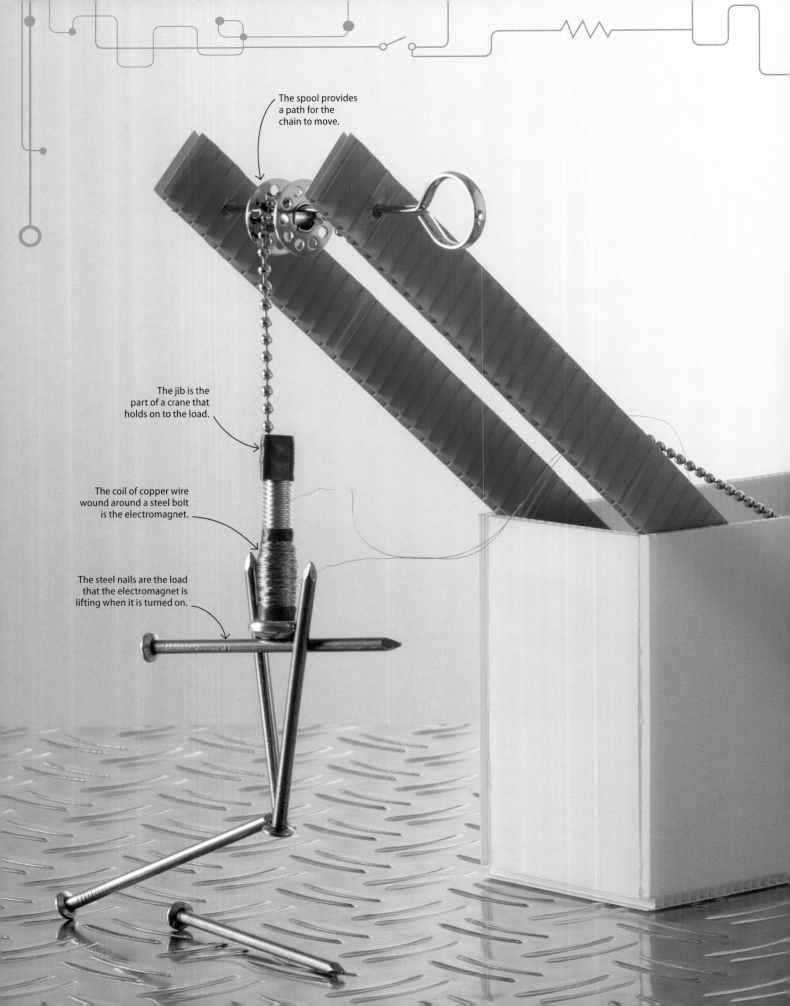

The spool provides
a path for the
chain to move.

The jib is the
part of a crane that
holds on to the load.

The coil of copper wire
wound around a steel bolt
is the electromagnet.

The steel nails are the load
that the electromagnet is
lifting when it is turned on.

Electromagnetic crane

Whenever an electric current flows through a wire, it causes the wire to become slightly magnetic. Wind a current-carrying wire into a coil and you have an electromagnet, which works just the same as an ordinary magnet, except that you can turn it on and off! Electric motors, computer hard drives, and loudspeakers are just some of the familiar devices that contain electromagnets. In this project, you'll make a crane that uses an electromagnet to lift steel objects.

Flicking the switch turns the electromagnet off.

Winding this metal skewer lifts or drops the crane's jib.

How to make an
Electromagnetic crane

The key to this build is to make it as strong as possible, so you can test the strength of the crane by lifting a heavy load. We have used corrugated plastic sheets to make the box, but you can use a similar material as long as it is sturdy. We have used a metal chain to support the crane's jib – if you can't get hold of one, you could use string or wire.

Time
45 mins

Be aware
Requires bradawl, hot-glue gun, and heat-shrink tubing use.

Difficulty
Easy

What you need

From the toolbox:

- Ruler
- Utility knife
- Cutting mat
- Bradawl
- Adhesive putty
- Hot-glue gun
- Marker
- Wire cutters
- Electrical tape
- Sandpaper
- Wire strippers
- Double-sided tape

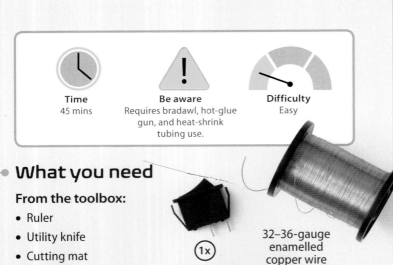

1x
SPST switch

32–36-gauge enamelled copper wire
28 m (8 ft 8½ in)

1x
Bolt 50 mm (2 in)

1x
Battery snap connector

1x
Piece of heat-shrink tubing

1x
Box
At least 13 x 10 x 6 cm
(5⅛ x 4 x 2⅜ in)

1x
Corrugated plastic sheet

1x
Grill lighter

1x
9-volt battery

2x
Metal skewers
15 cm (6 in)

1x
Metal chain
1 m (3 ft)

1x
Metal bobbin

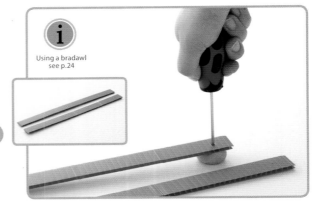

Using a bradawl see p.24

1 Cut two strips of corrugated plastic 30 cm (12 in) by 2 cm (¾ in). Use the bradawl to make a hole in the centre of each strip about 2½ cm (1 in) from one of the ends.

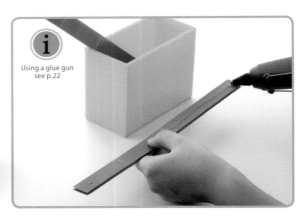

Using a glue gun see p.22

2 Glue the strips to the inside of the box. Make sure the two holes at the top are aligned.

You can glue around the holes to secure the skewer in place if you like.

3 Place one of the metal skewers through one of the holes, slip the metal bobbin on to the skewer, then stick the skewer through the other hole.

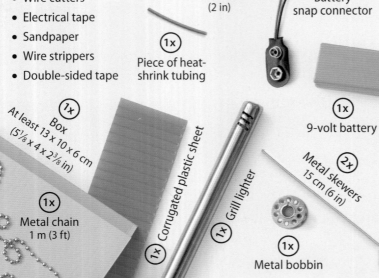

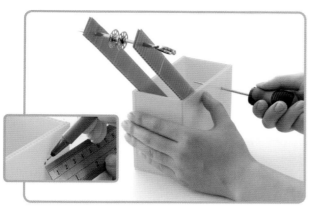

4 Mark a dot 2 cm (¾ in) down and 3 cm (1⅛ in) in from the opposite corner of the box on both sides, as shown. Use the bradawl to poke a hole through both dots.

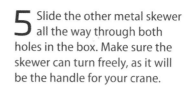

5 Slide the other metal skewer all the way through both holes in the box. Make sure the skewer can turn freely, as it will be the handle for your crane.

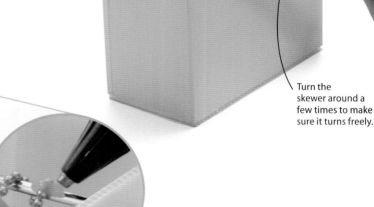

Turn the skewer around a few times to make sure it turns freely.

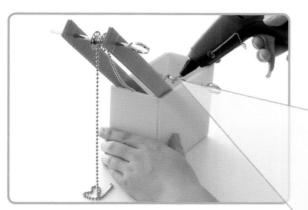

6 Wrap the end of the chain around the middle of the lower skewer, and secure it in place with some hot glue. When the glue has dried, spin the skewer to wrap the length of the chain around it.

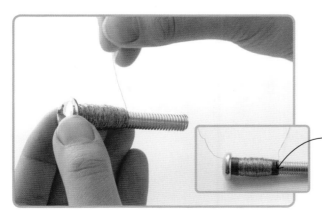

Tape the coil to the bolt to secure it in place.

7 Next, starting at least 15 cm (6 in) in from one end, wrap the enamelled copper wire tightly around the bolt about 600 times. Cut the wire, leaving another 15 cm (6 in) free at the other end.

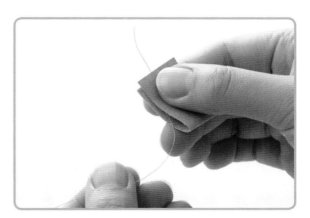

8 Use the sandpaper to scrape 2½ cm (1 in) of the coating off both ends of the enamelled wire to reveal the shiny copper. This will allow you to make an electrical connection at each end.

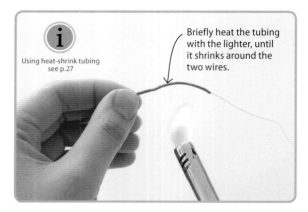

Using heat-shrink tubing see p.27

Briefly heat the tubing with the lighter, until it shrinks around the two wires.

9 Strip the battery snap connector wires. Slip some heat-shrink tubing over one of the copper wires, and wrap the wire around one of the battery wires. Cover the joint with the tubing and heat-shrink it.

10 Wrap the other end of the copper wire around one of the terminals on the switch. If you want to make it more secure, you can solder it in place, but it is not necessary.

11 Wrap the remaining wire from the battery snap connector to the other terminal of the switch. Again, if you wish to make it more secure, you can solder it in place.

12 Now, take the bolt from step 7. Tape the free end of the metal chain securely to the smaller end of the bolt.

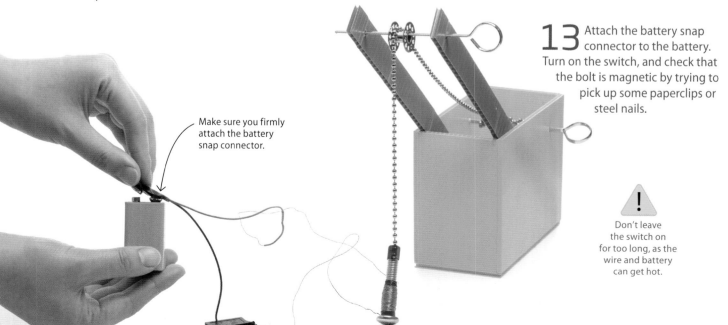

Make sure you firmly attach the battery snap connector.

13 Attach the battery snap connector to the battery. Turn on the switch, and check that the bolt is magnetic by trying to pick up some paperclips or steel nails.

⚠

Don't leave the switch on for too long, as the wire and battery can get hot.

14 Turn off the switch, and use the double-sided tape to stick the battery and the switch inside the box. Your electromagnetic crane is ready!

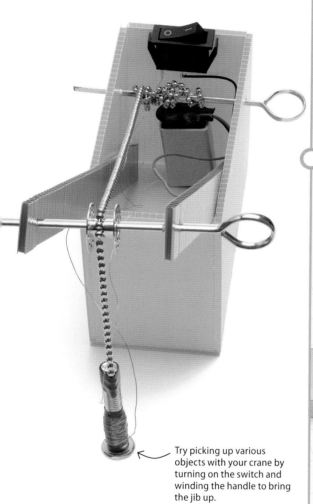

Try picking up various objects with your crane by turning on the switch and winding the handle to bring the jib up.

How it works

When an electric current is flowing, a magnetic field is created. The stronger the current, the stronger the magnetic field. In your electromagnetic crane, this effect is increased by coiling the wire and adding the bolt. This increased magnetic field attracts the steel nails.

1. A magnetic field surrounds the wire when a current is running through it.

2. When the wire is coiled, the magnetic field becomes more powerful. Adding more turns increases the strength of the field.

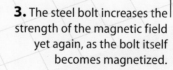

3. The steel bolt increases the strength of the magnetic field yet again, as the bolt itself becomes magnetized.

Real-world inventions
Scrap-metal crane

Large, powerful electromagnetic cranes are used in scrapyards to pick up scrap metal. It only works on ferrous metals – those containing iron. Since most scrap metal is steel, which is a combination of iron and carbon, these cranes are perfect tools. Similar cranes are used in factories to move large sheets of steel around.

When the door opens, the craft stick is jerked out of the teeth of the clip, completing the circuit.

These nuts attached to a motor spin and strike the bell when the circuit is completed.

Door alarm

Frighten intruders away from your room with this mechanical door alarm, which rings out when someone trips the system. All the trespasser needs to do is open the door: this causes an electrical circuit to complete, which triggers two metal nuts to repeatedly strike a bell, alerting everyone nearby!

How to make a
Door alarm

In this project, you'll need to screw into a door frame – so make sure you ask permission first! We have used a call bell that we've taken apart, but anything that makes a ringing noise when struck will work. You also need a bolt to hold the bell slightly above the base.

Time 45 mins	**Be aware** Requires drill, soldering iron, and hot-glue gun use.	**Difficulty** Medium

What you need

From the toolbox:

- Drill and drill bit
- Scrap wood and clamps
- Ruler
- Wire strippers
- Wire cutters
- Soldering iron and solder
- Hot-glue gun
- Double-sided foam tape

(1x) SPST switch

(1x) Bolt

(1x) Battery snap connector

(1x) Bell bowl

(1x) Screw

(1x) 6-volt motor

(2x) AA batteries

(1x) Clip

(9x) Nuts

(1x) 3-volt battery pack

(1x) A6-sized base board

(1x) Chain

(1x) Craft stick

Black stranded wire 20 cm (8 in)

Drilling see p.23

Use a piece of scrap wood to protect your work surface.

1 Use a drill bit that is slightly wider than the diameter of your bell bolt to drill a hole in the base board about 5 cm (2 in) from two edges.

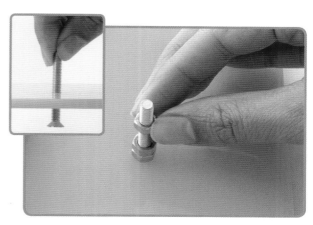

2 Slide the bolt upwards through the hole and screw three nuts all the way down the bolt to hold it in place.

3 Place the bell upside down on top of the three nuts and secure it with another nut.

Use clamps to hold the base board in place when drilling.

4 Drill a 3 mm (⅛ in) hole about 4 cm (1½ in) from the rim of the bell, in line with the bolt. This will create a seat for the motor to rest in.

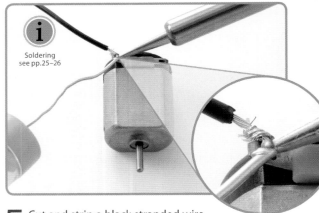

Soldering see pp.25–26

5 Cut and strip a black stranded wire about 10 cm (4 in) long. Twist it around one of the motor terminals and then solder it in place.

It doesn't matter which terminal you solder to as either end can be open or closed on a SPST switch.

6 Solder the other end of the wire to one of the SPST switch terminals.

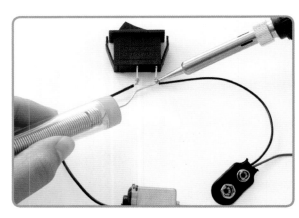

7 Strip about 3 cm (1⅛ in) of insulation off the red wire on the battery snap connector. Strip and solder the black wire to the remaining SPST switch terminal.

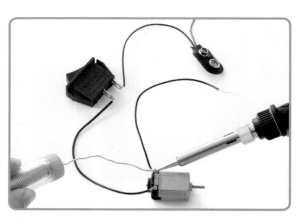

8 Cut and strip both ends of a black stranded wire about 10 cm (4 in) long, taking about 3 cm (1⅛ in) of insulation off one end. Solder the other end of this wire to the remaining motor terminal.

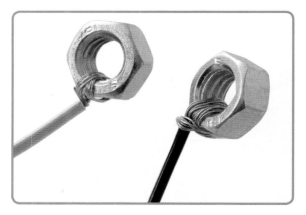

9 Wrap the bared end of the red wire from the battery snap connector around a nut, and the black wire attached to the motor around another nut. Make sure each nut is tightly secured to each wire.

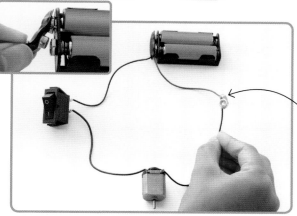

You might see a little spark when the nuts come near each other.

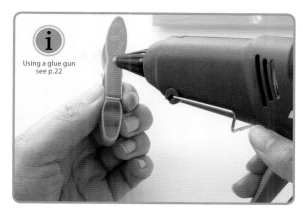

Using a glue gun see p.22

10 Insert the batteries into the battery pack and connect the snap connector. Test the circuit by flipping the SPST switch: the motor should whirr when you touch the two nuts together. Turn the switch off.

11 Apply hot glue to one side of the clip, and stick it onto the base board, so that the mouth of the clip is roughly in line with the battery pack.

12 Next, use the hot-glue gun to glue the battery, switch, and motor onto the base board. Glue the motor directly over the hole you drilled in step 4 – but make sure no glue gets near the motor's shaft.

Turning the switch on readies the alarm, but no current will flow to the motor until the two nuts touch.

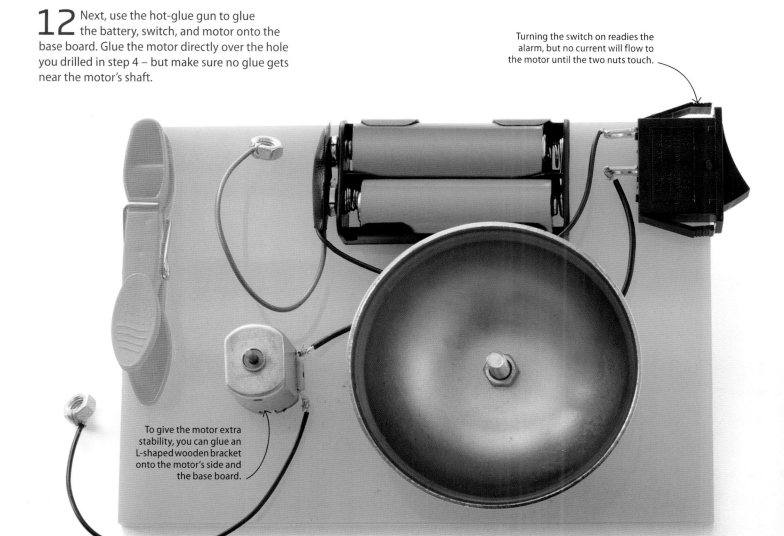

To give the motor extra stability, you can glue an L-shaped wooden bracket onto the motor's side and the base board.

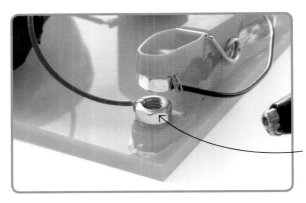

Carefully glue the nuts one at a time, so they don't end up glued together.

13 Take the two wired nuts from step 9 and glue one each to the upper and lower jaw on the clip's mouth.

14 Take another nut and glue one side of it to the top of the motor shaft. Be careful not to let glue drip down into the motor, and make sure the hole in the middle of the nut is clear.

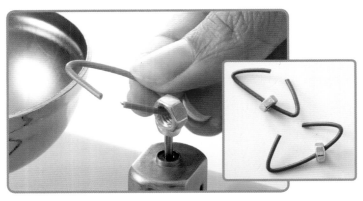

15 Cut two wires into equal lengths, which, when bent in half, are long enough to reach the motor shaft and bell. Thread the wires through a nut each and then bend each wire into a "U" shape.

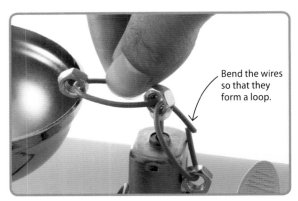

Bend the wires so that they form a loop.

16 Thread the wires with the nuts through the motor nut. Adjust the length of the wires to ensure that the nuts can reach the edge of the bell.

17 Now glue the wire loops closed. Each wire loop should have a nut on it, and each of these nuts should be able to hit the bell when the motor turns.

Clamp the stick to a piece of scrap wood before drilling.

18 Cut the craft stick in half, then drill a hole near the end of one half. Attach one end of the chain to the hole, and secure the other end to the door frame with a screw (ask permission first!).

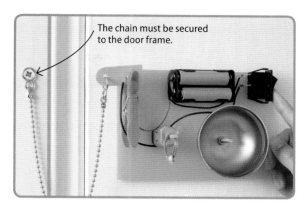

The chain must be secured to the door frame.

19 Use double-sided foam tape to fix the alarm to the door. Place the craft stick between the nuts in the clip's jaw.

20 Flip the switch. The next time the door is opened, the craft stick will slide out of the clip, causing the circuit to complete and the alarm to sound.

Open circuit

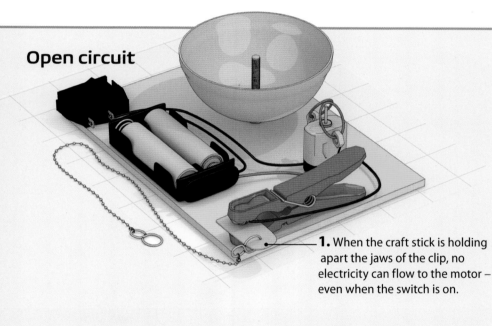

1. When the craft stick is holding apart the jaws of the clip, no electricity can flow to the motor – even when the switch is on.

Closed circuit

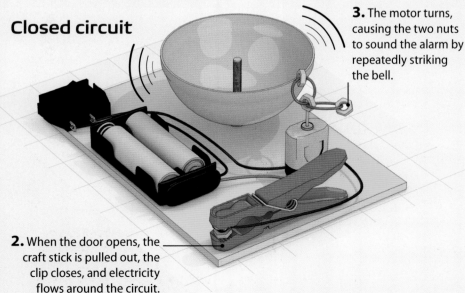

3. The motor turns, causing the two nuts to sound the alarm by repeatedly striking the bell.

2. When the door opens, the craft stick is pulled out, the clip closes, and electricity flows around the circuit.

How it works

The piece of craft stick is made of wood, which does not conduct electricity, and when it is removed, the circuit is complete.

Real-world inventions
Refrigerator light

When you open a refrigerator door, the light inside the refrigerator comes on automatically. There is a spring-loaded switch just inside the door that is off when the door is closed. When you open the door, it causes the switch's contacts to complete a circuit, which turns the light on.

Infinity mirror

How can you make a normal mirror look like it stretches on forever? All you need to achieve this illusion is a strip of LED lights, some mirrored film, a picture frame, and a mirror. The lights from the LED strip are reflected again and again inside the frame, creating images that appear to fade far into the distance!

Each reflection of the LED strip is dimmer and smaller than the last one, which gives the effect of great depth.

How to make an
Infinity mirror

For this project, you will need a "deep-box" frame with a removable inner frame. Any size frame will work, but the mirror must fit perfectly into the outer frame. Either match the frame's size to the mirror's size, or get the mirror cut by a professional to match the frame. Finally, be careful handling the mirror and glass as they can cut you.

Time
20 mins

Be aware
Requires utility knife, drill, and mains electricity use.

Difficulty
Easy

What you need

From the toolbox:

- Utility knife
- Cutting mat
- Ruler
- Drill
- 8 mm (⁵⁄₁₆ in) drill bit
- Scissors

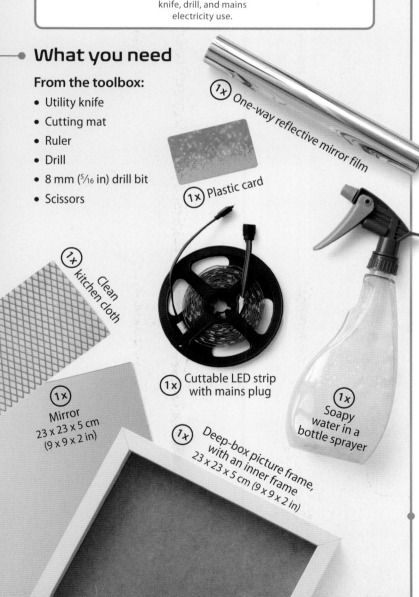

1x One-way reflective mirror film

1x Plastic card

1x Clean kitchen cloth

1x Cuttable LED strip with mains plug

1x Soapy water in a bottle sprayer

1x Mirror
23 x 23 x 5 cm
(9 x 9 x 2 in)

1x Deep-box picture frame, with an inner frame,
23 x 23 x 5 cm (9 x 9 x 2 in)

Utility knife
see p.20

1 Remove the glass or plastic window from the frame. Use it as a template to cut the one-way mirror film so that it is slightly wider than the window on all sides. If the window has a protective covering, peel it off.

2 Lay the window on a flat surface and spray it with a little soapy water. The water will help the one-way mirror film to stick to the window.

Use both hands to ensure the mirror film doesn't stick to itself.

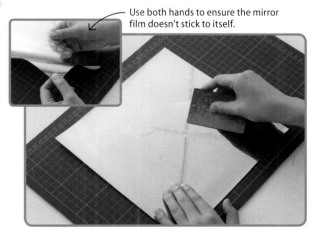

3 Carefully peel off the mirror film's backing. Place the adhesive side of the mirror film onto the window. Working out from the centre, use the plastic card to smooth any bubbles out to create a flat surface.

Use a metal ruler to protect your fingers when cutting.

4 Dry the window with a towel, then trim off the excess mirror film with a utility knife.

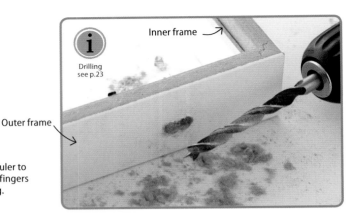

Inner frame

i Drilling see p.23

Outer frame

5 Drill a hole through the outer and inner frames. Make it wide enough to accommodate the cord of the LED strip. You may need to drill two holes side by side to allow for this.

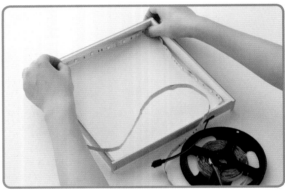

6 Remove the inner frame, and measure the LED strip so there is enough to go around the entire length of the inner frame's inside.

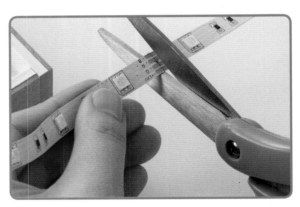

7 Cut the LED strip. Make sure you only cut the strip on the marked cut lines.

8 Feed the end of the LED strip through the drilled hole in the inner frame.

9 Stick the adhesive side of the LED strip inside the inner frame, removing the backing as you go. If your LED strip doesn't have adhesive backing, use hot glue or double-sided tape.

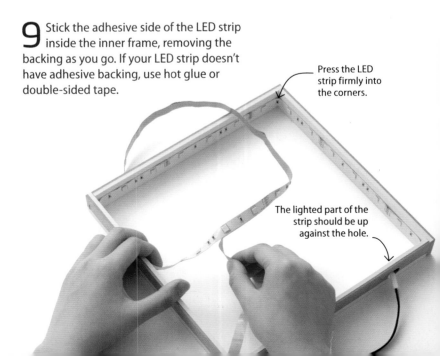

Press the LED strip firmly into the corners.

The lighted part of the strip should be up against the hole.

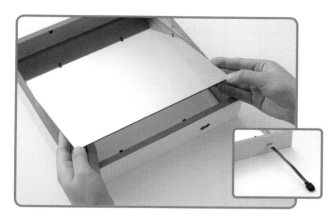

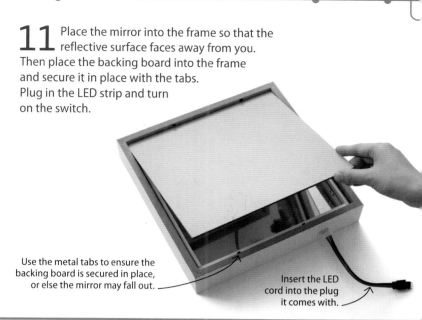

11 Place the mirror into the frame so that the reflective surface faces away from you. Then place the backing board into the frame and secure it in place with the tabs. Plug in the LED strip and turn on the switch.

Use the metal tabs to ensure the backing board is secured in place, or else the mirror may fall out.

Insert the LED cord into the plug it comes with.

10 Lay the window into the outer frame with the mirror film facing towards you. Feed the cord from the LED strip through the drilled hole in the outer frame, and lay the inner frame on top of the window.

How it works

Your infinity mirror works by bouncing the light from the LEDs off the mirror and the mirror film again and again, which gives the impression of an infinite depth to the mirror.

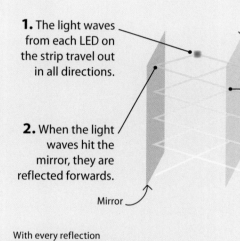

Mirror film

1. The light waves from each LED on the strip travel out in all directions.

2. When the light waves hit the mirror, they are reflected forwards.

Mirror

3. When this reflected light hits the mirror film at the front of the frame, half the light reflects back in and half the light passes straight through, allowing it to be seen.

With every reflection in the mirror, the LED appears dimmer as light is lost through the mirror film.

4. The reflected light reflects off the back mirror and the mirror film again and again, forming multiple images of the LED, each one appearing smaller and further back than the last one, giving the illusion of depth.

LED

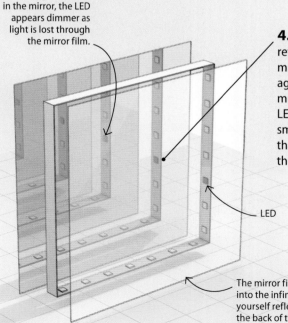

The mirror film allows you to look into the infinity mirror, and see yourself reflected in the mirror at the back of the picture frame.

Real-world inventions
One-way mirrors

Some police interview rooms have a half-mirrored window like the window at the front of your infinity mirror. To people inside the interview room, it looks like a mirror – but people watching in the next room can see through it, like a window.

AM radio

With just a handful of components and a bit of know-how, you can catch the airwaves by making your own radio. "AM" stands for "amplitude modulation", which is one way to send a radio signal. AM signals can travel over great distances, and were the first kind of signals used for broadcasting radio signals.

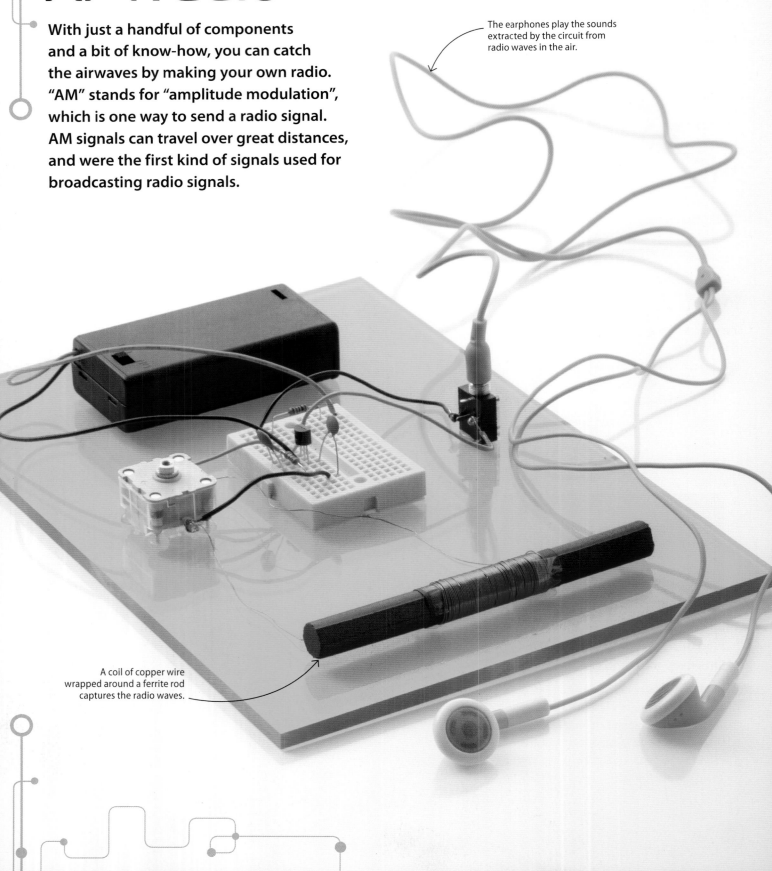

The earphones play the sounds extracted by the circuit from radio waves in the air.

A coil of copper wire wrapped around a ferrite rod captures the radio waves.

How to make an
AM radio

Make sure the earphone socket is the right fit for your earphones or headphones. You'll need to use a soldering iron in several parts of the project, so make sure you work somewhere where you can leave it plugged in safely.

Time
40 mins

Be aware
Requires soldering iron and hot-glue gun use.

Difficulty
Medium

What you need

From the toolbox:

- Ruler
- Clear tape
- Wire cutters
- Sandpaper
- Third-hand tool
- Soldering iron and solder
- Wire strippers
- Pliers
- Multimeter
- Hot-glue gun

30 gauge
enamelled copper wire
2¾ m (9 ft)

(1x) Earphone socket

(1x) Variable tuning capacitor

(1x) 100 kΩ resistor

(1x) 1 kΩ resistor

(1x) Ferrite rod

(1x) A5 base

(1x) Earphones or headphones

(2x) AA batteries

(1x) 0.1 µF capacitor

(1x) 3-volt battery pack with wires

(1x) TA7642 AM radio IC

(1x) Mini breadboard

(1x) 0.01 µF capacitor

Black solid-core wire
18 cm (7⅛ in)

Red solid-core wire
18 cm (7⅛ in)

1 Tape the copper wire to the ferrite rod, leaving about 10 cm (4 in) of wire on the end. Next, wind the wire around the rod, making about 80 turns. Cut the wire, leaving about 10 cm (4 in) at the other end, and secure it with tape.

The ferrite rod makes the coil more sensitive to radio waves.

2 Use sandpaper to remove about 2½ cm (1 in) of the coating at each end of the copper wire. This will reveal shiny copper, which will allow you to make an electrical connection at each end.

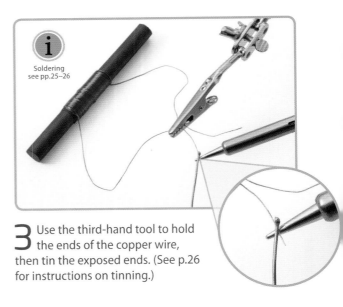

Soldering
see pp.25–26

3 Use the third-hand tool to hold the ends of the copper wire, then tin the exposed ends. (See p.26 for instructions on tinning.)

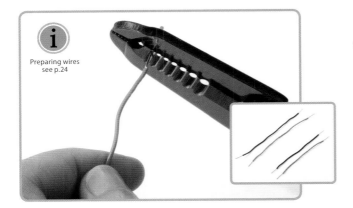

Preparing wires
see p.24

4 Cut a red wire and a black wire each at 8 cm (3⅛ in) long, then another pair each at 10 cm (4 in) long. Use wire strippers to strip about 1 cm (⅜ in) off each end of all four wires.

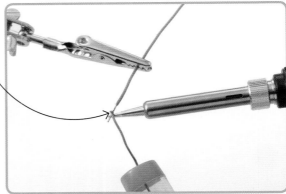

The solder on the tinned ends will melt when you attach the wires.

5 Use solder and a soldering iron to tin one end of each of the four wires. The tinned ends of the wires will connect both the tuning capacitor and the headphone socket to the circuit board.

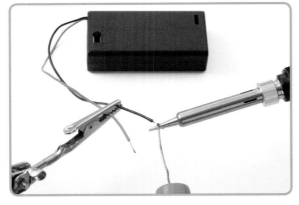

6 Trim the ends of the battery pack wires and strip about 1 cm (⅜ in) off the ends. Twist the stranded wires and tin these too, using the third-hand tool to hold the wires in place.

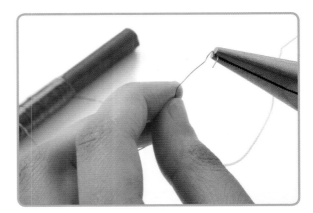

7 Use the needle-nose pliers to bend the tinned ends of the copper coil wire back on themselves, forming small hooks.

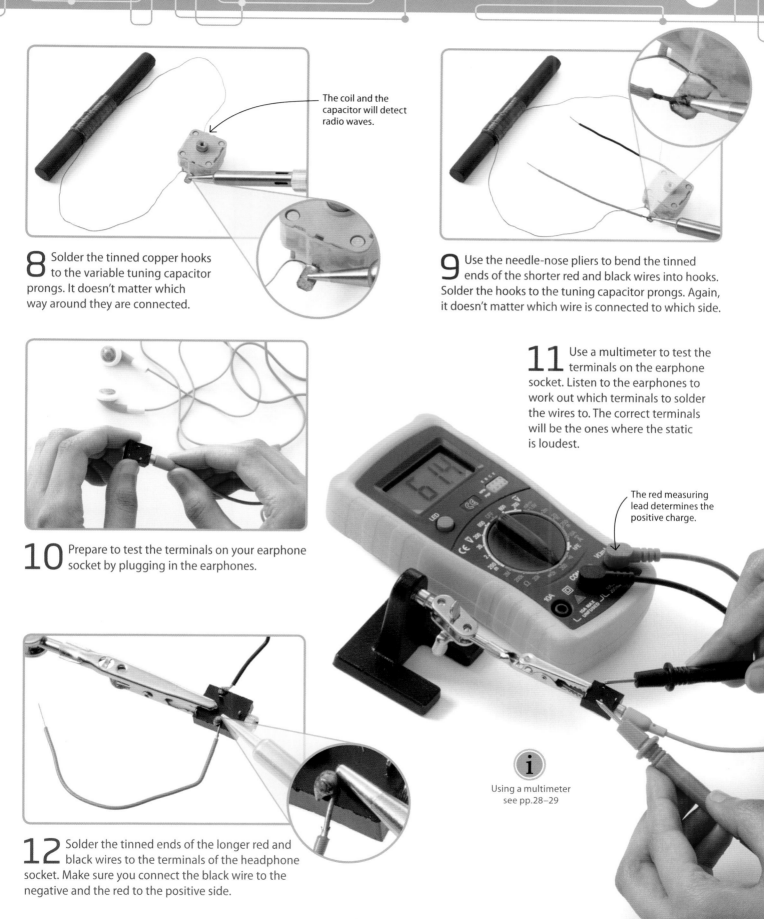

The coil and the capacitor will detect radio waves.

8 Solder the tinned copper hooks to the variable tuning capacitor prongs. It doesn't matter which way around they are connected.

9 Use the needle-nose pliers to bend the tinned ends of the shorter red and black wires into hooks. Solder the hooks to the tuning capacitor prongs. Again, it doesn't matter which wire is connected to which side.

11 Use a multimeter to test the terminals on the earphone socket. Listen to the earphones to work out which terminals to solder the wires to. The correct terminals will be the ones where the static is loudest.

The red measuring lead determines the positive charge.

10 Prepare to test the terminals on your earphone socket by plugging in the earphones.

12 Solder the tinned ends of the longer red and black wires to the terminals of the headphone socket. Make sure you connect the black wire to the negative and the red to the positive side.

Using a multimeter
see pp.28–29

13 Follow this breadboard map to plug all of the individual components into the mini breadboard. Make sure the flat side of the TA7642 AM radio IC faces in towards the middle of the breadboard.

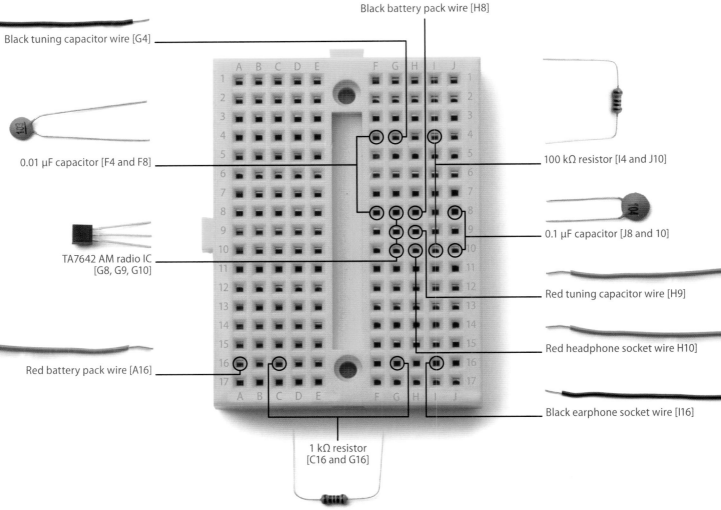

Black battery pack wire [H8]

Black tuning capacitor wire [G4]

0.01 µF capacitor [F4 and F8]

TA7642 AM radio IC [G8, G9, G10]

Red battery pack wire [A16]

100 kΩ resistor [I4 and J10]

0.1 µF capacitor [J8 and 10]

Red tuning capacitor wire [H9]

Red headphone socket wire H10]

Black earphone socket wire [I16]

1 kΩ resistor [C16 and G16]

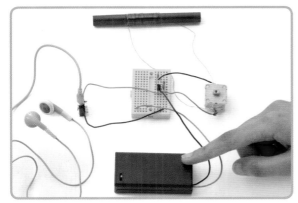

14 Plug in the earphones, and insert the batteries into the battery pack. If the circuit is working, you will hear static noise through the earphones.

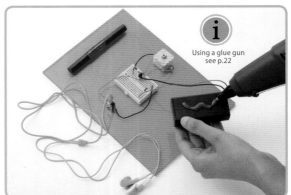

15 If you can't hear any static, check all the connections. Once you hear the static, glue down all the components to the base. Tune the knob on the tuning capacitor to pick up AM radio stations.

How it works

AM stands for "amplitude modulation". "Amplitude" means the height of a wave, and "modulation" means to change something. AM radio stations take a base carrier wave and change its amplitude to carry sounds, which they then broadcast at a specific address on the radio wave spectrum, called a station's frequency. These waves enter your AM radio through the coil.

Real-world inventions
FM and DAB

Starting in the 1920s, the first radio stations used AM technology, but a rival method of broadcasting, called frequency modulation (FM), overtook it by the end of the 20th century. These days, many radio stations use digital audio broadcasting (DAB), which relies on computers to create the signals they beam out.

1. Radio waves create an electric current in your AM radio coil that is an exact copy of the original electrical signal.

2. When you select one of these signals with the tuning capacitor, it passes to the TA7642 AM radio IC.

You can turn the knob on the tuning capacitor to pick up different radio stations.

4. The earphones then convert the audio signal into sound waves.

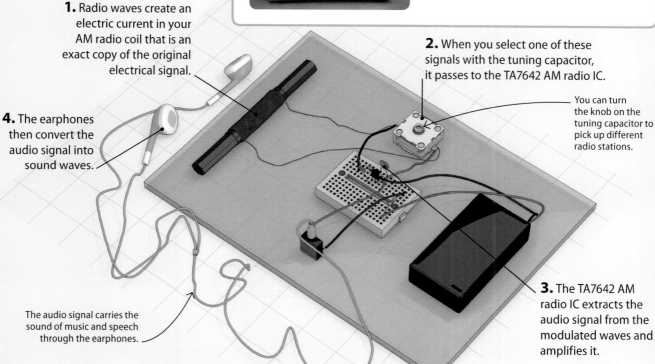

The audio signal carries the sound of music and speech through the earphones.

3. The TA7642 AM radio IC extracts the audio signal from the modulated waves and amplifies it.

Different radio stations release sound as radio waves.

The coil picks up the radio waves, and you use the tuning capacitor to select a particular frequency.

The TA7642 AM radio IC amplifies the signal.

The fixed capacitor smooths out the signal to become a clear audio signal.

The earphones turn the audio signal into sound so you can hear the original sounds.

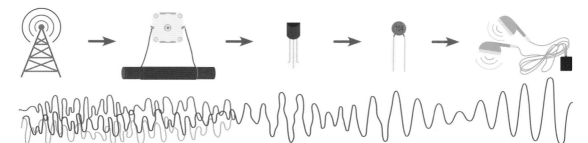

Many AM radio signals

Specific but unclear radio signal

Specific and clear radio signal

Bend the copper wire into simple or complicated shapes.

The switch allows you to turn the game off when you are not using it.

Inside the box are a battery and a buzzer.

Buzzer game

Do you have a steady hand? Find out by making this game! Try manoeuvring the copper loop from one end of the twisting path to the other without the loop and wire touching. If they do, a buzzer will sound and an LED will light up to let you know that you've lost the game. Challenge your friends and see who can get the furthest.

How to make a
Buzzer game

Before you start this project, you'll need to prepare the sides of the box. Ask an adult to help you cut out five squares from plastic or wood. Most buzzers will work at a range of voltages from about 3 volts to 20 volts – this circuit uses a 9-volt battery.

Time
60 mins

Be aware
Requires drill, hot-glue gun, and soldering iron use.

Difficulty
Hard

What you need

From the toolbox

- Drill
- Scrap wood and clamps
- 3 mm (⅛ in) drill bit
- 8 mm (⁵⁄₁₆ in) drill bit
- Sandpaper
- Hot-glue gun
- Wire strippers
- Soldering iron and solder
- Wire cutters
- Pliers
- Electrical tape

1x
9-volt battery

1x
SPST switch

1x
330 Ω resistor

1x
Battery snap connector

Thick unlaquered copper wire
1 m 15 cm (3 ft 9 in)

1x
Buzzer

1x
LED

5x
10 x 10 cm
(4 x 4 in) panels

Black stranded wire
50 cm (19¾ in)

Red stranded wire
6 cm (2⅜ in)

ⓘ Drilling see p.23

1 Using the 3 mm (⅛ in) drill bit, make a hole for the LED's legs in the centre of one of the box sides. Drill two more holes big enough to fit the copper wire, each 1 cm (⅜ in) from the LED hole.

2 On another box side, use the 3 mm (⅛ in) drill bit to make a hole in the corner. In a different corner, use the 8 mm (⁵⁄₁₆ in) drill bit to create a rectangular slot large enough for the switch to sit in. Use sandpaper to smooth the slot.

3 Use a hot-glue gun to join four panels together along their sides as shown below.

The side with the three holes will be the top of your box.

ⓘ Using a glue gun see p.22

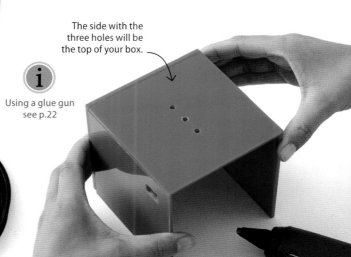

4 Slot the SPST switch and the LED into their holes. Once through, widen the legs of the LED against the inside of the box to secure it in place.

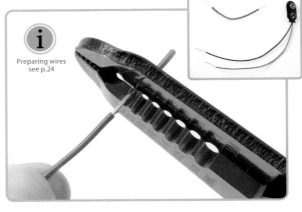

ℹ Preparing wires see p.24

5 Cut and strip a piece of red stranded wire approximately 6 cm (2⅜ in) long. Next, strip the battery snap connector wires.

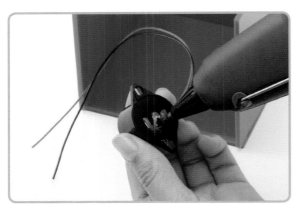

6 Tip the box on its side, so you can see into it. Glue the buzzer near the bottom of one side, near enough to connect it to the switch.

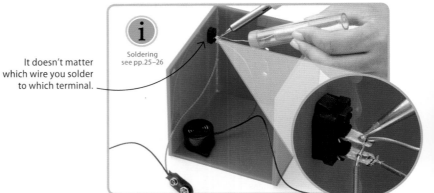

It doesn't matter which wire you solder to which terminal.

ℹ Soldering see pp.25–26

7 Strip the end of the buzzer's red wire. Twist the red battery snap connector wire around one switch terminal, and the red buzzer wire around the other terminal. Solder both in place.

8 Solder one end of the red stranded wire from step 5 onto the same switch terminal as the red buzzer wire.

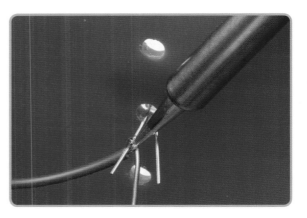

9 Solder the other end of the stranded wire to the shorter (negative) leg of the LED.

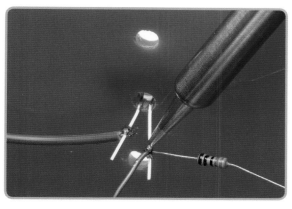

10 Solder one end of the resistor (it doesn't matter which end) onto the longer leg of the LED. Make sure the two legs of the LED are not touching.

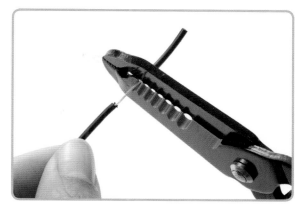

11 Strip about 3½ cm (1⅜ in) from the black buzzer wire. This wire will wrap around a resistor and one end of the copper wire.

You can solder the resistor to the black buzzer wire for extra stability if you wish.

12 Twist the other end of the resistor firmly around the black buzzer. Leave about 2 cm (¾ in) of stripped wire left over.

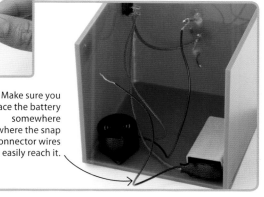

Make sure you place the battery somewhere where the snap connector wires can easily reach it.

13 Attach the battery to the snap connector. Glue the LED and switch securely into their slots and glue the battery anywhere inside the box.

14 Cut about 1 m (3¼ ft) of the thick copper wire. Use the pliers to twist the wire into whatever shape you like. Make sure you keep the last 2½ cm (1 in) of each end of the wire straight.

The more twists, turns, and loops you add, the more challenging the game will be.

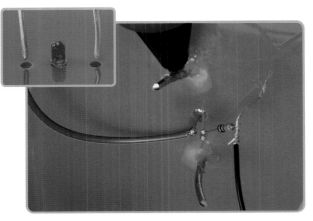

15 Insert the two ends of the copper wire into the holes on the top of the box, and glue them into place. Make sure there is about 1 cm (³⁄₈ in) of each end sticking into the box.

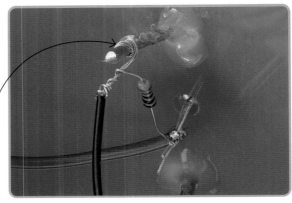

Twist the wire tightly around the copper wire and solder if needed to secure it.

16 Twist the end of the buzzer's black wire firmly around one of the ends of copper wire inside the box.

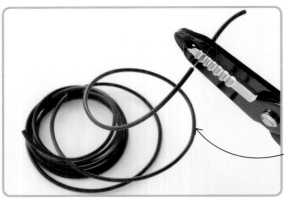

The wire should be long enough to reach from the bottom of the box over the copper wire shape.

17 Cut a piece of black stranded wire about 50 cm (19³⁄₄ in) long. Strip about 1 cm (³⁄₈ in) off one end and about 3¹⁄₂ cm (1³⁄₈ in) off the other.

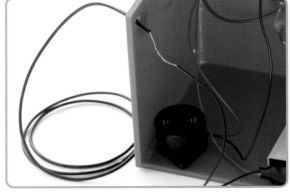

18 Thread the shorter stripped end of the black wire through the remaining hole in the side of the box, and twist it around the black battery wire.

19 Cut another piece of the copper wire, about 15 cm (5⁷⁄₈ in) long. Use the pliers to bend the end into a loop.

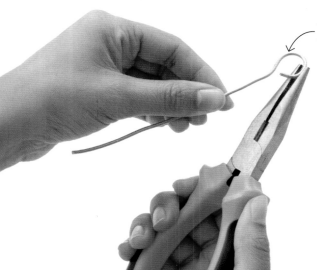

The tighter the loop, the more difficult the game will be.

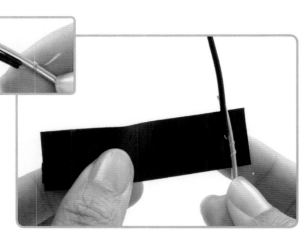

20 Twist the stripped end of the long black wire around the straight end of the copper loop. Secure the wire connection by wrapping electrical tape tightly around it.

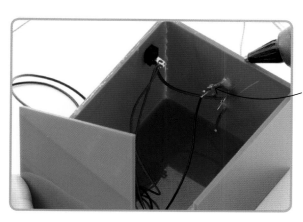

Be careful to ensure no glue goes on the circuit inside.

21 Use hot glue to attach the final panel to the side of the box. The bottom of the box should be left open.

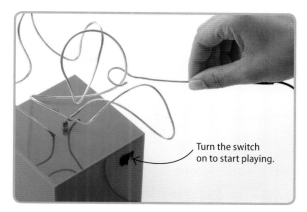

Turn the switch on to start playing.

22 Your buzzer game is finished. Slide the loop onto the copper wire to play. See if you can get the wire loop from one end of the copper wire to the other. If the loop touches the wire, the buzzer will sound and the LED will light up, and you have failed.

How it works

If you keep the copper loop away from the copper wire, the circuit is incomplete. No current flows, the buzzer will not make a sound, and the LED will not light up. This means you're winning!

2. When the circuit is complete, current flows through the resistor and the LED, lighting the LED. Some current also flows through the buzzer, making it buzz loudly, letting you know you have failed.

1. When the loop touches the wire, you are completing the circuit.

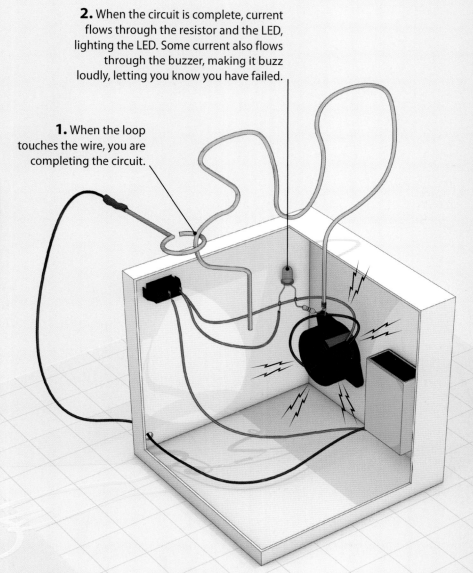

Real-world inventions
Bumper cars
Inside a bumper car is an electric motor that powers the wheels and electric lights for headlamps. The floor and the ceiling of the ride are connected to an electrical power supply. A metal pole touches the ceiling, and a metal contact beneath the car touches the floor. Electric current flows through the motor and the lights, as long as you have the foot pedal pressed down.

Breadboard car

This speedy car is powered by nothing more
than a simple household battery. All you'll
need to do is connect a few wires and simple
components on a breadboard – which also
acts as the car's frame. The car has bright LEDs
as its headlamps and a motor that turns a
propeller to make the car move.

The breadboard makes it
easier to wire the circuit as
components and wires can
simply be inserted into it.

The battery supplies
electric current to
the circuit.

A resistor ensures that
just the right amount of
electric current flows
through the LEDs.

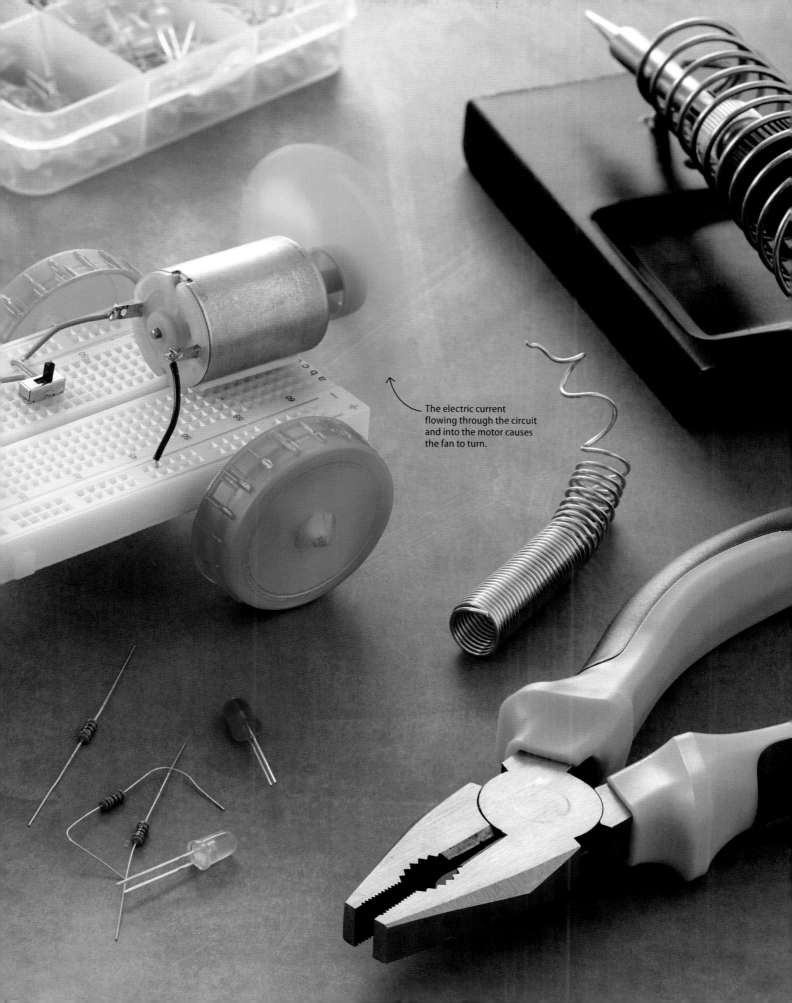

The electric current flowing through the circuit and into the motor causes the fan to turn.

How to make a
Breadboard car

You'll need to follow these steps carefully to make sure you wire up the LEDs and the motor correctly. The motor is powered by a 9-volt battery: if it becomes hot, switch off the car for a few minutes to let it cool down. For more information on how breadboards work, see pp.34–35.

Time
35 mins

Be aware
Requires hot-glue gun and soldering iron use.

Difficulty
Medium

What you need

From the toolbox:

- Ruler
- Scissors
- Hot-glue gun
- Wire cutters
- Double-sided foam tape
- Wire strippers
- Pliers
- Soldering iron and solder

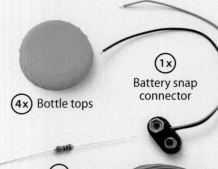

(4x) Bottle tops

(1x) Battery snap connector

(1x) 510 Ω resistor

Red solid-core wire
6 cm (2⅜ in)

(1x) 3–9-volt motor

(1x) Plastic propeller

(2x) Skewers

(1x) SPST switch

Black solid-core wire
4 cm (1½ in)

(2x) Red LEDs

(2x) Straws

(1x) 840-pin breadboard

(1x) 9-volt battery

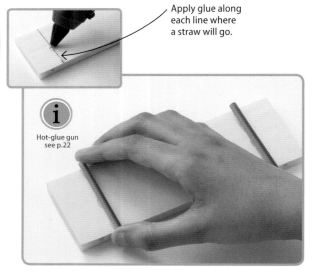

> Apply glue along each line where a straw will go.

i Hot-glue gun see p.22

1 Mark two lines on the bottom of your breadboard that are at equal distances from the ends. Cut two lengths from the straws, each slightly wider than the breadboard. Use hot glue to stick the straws down.

2 Use the sharp end of a skewer to poke a hole through the centre of each of the bottle tops. Take care not to hurt yourself with the sharp point.

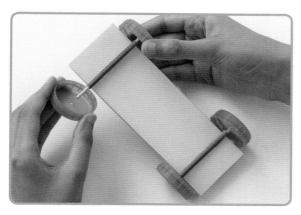

3 Trim two skewers so that they are about 3 cm (1⅛ in) longer than the straws. Slide the skewers through the straws and push one bottle top onto each side of each skewer, as shown.

4 Put a small amount of glue on the ends of the skewers to hold the wheels in place. Make sure the wheels are at right angles to the skewer.

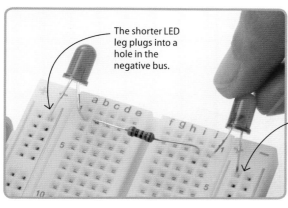

The shorter LED leg plugs into a hole in the negative bus.

The longer LED leg plugs into a hole in the positive bus.

5 Plug in the LEDs and resistor as shown. It doesn't matter which way around the resistor goes. Carefully bend the LED legs forward at right angles to look like headlights.

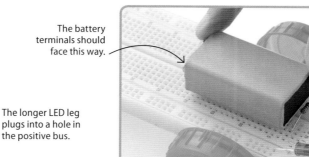

The battery terminals should face this way.

6 Cut a piece of double-sided foam tape the same size as your battery. Use it to secure the battery to the board, directly behind the resistor.

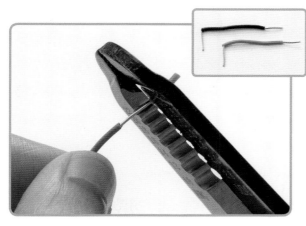

7 Cut a piece of black wire and a piece of red wire about 4 cm (1½ in) in length. Strip 1 cm (⅜ in) off the ends of each wire, and bend down the stripped end at one side of each wire.

8 Solder the non-bent end of the wires to the terminals on your motor.

ℹ
Soldering iron
see pp.25–26

The motor's shaft will hold the car's propeller.

The double-sided foam tape keeps the motor in place.

9 Cut a small piece of the double-sided foam tape and use it to secure the motor to the other end of the breadboard, with the motor's shaft pointing off the end of the breadboard.

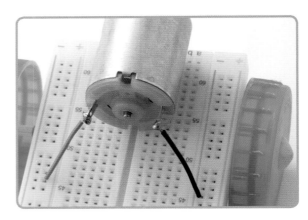

10 Plug the red wire into a hole in the closest positive bus and the black wire from your motor into a hole in the closest negative bus.

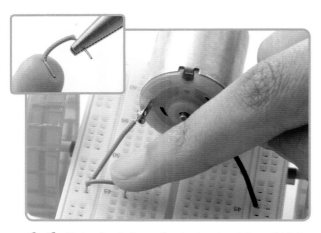

11 Cut a short piece of red wire about 2 cm (¾ in) long. Strip a little insulation off the ends, and bend the bared wire with your pliers. Push the ends into the breadboard as shown.

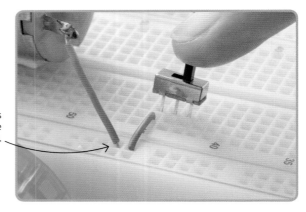

Make sure the ends of the wires are firmly in place.

12 Plug the SPST switch into the breadboard as shown. The first prong of the switch should be in the same row as the small red wire.

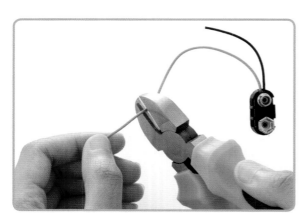

13 Connect the battery snap connector to the battery. Use the wire cutters to trim the wires of the snap connector. Strip about ½ cm (¼ in) off the ends of the wires and twist the bared ends.

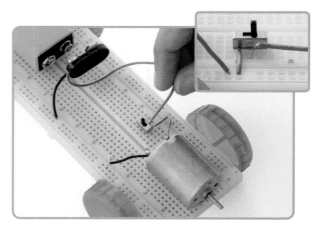

14 Push the end of the negative (black) wire into a hole in the negative bus and the end of the positive (red) wire into a hole next to the middle pin of the switch, as shown.

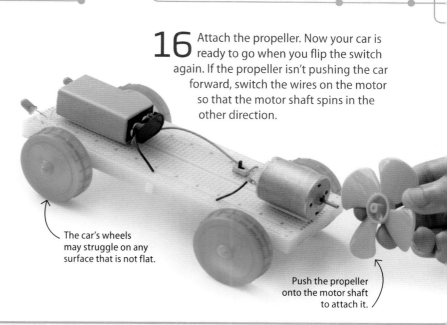

16 Attach the propeller. Now your car is ready to go when you flip the switch again. If the propeller isn't pushing the car forward, switch the wires on the motor so that the motor shaft spins in the other direction.

The car's wheels may struggle on any surface that is not flat.

Push the propeller onto the motor shaft to attach it.

15 Flip the switch to check that your circuit is working. If it is, the two LEDs will light up, and the motor will whirr. If not, go back and check the previous steps carefully.

How it works

When you flip the switch, you are completing the circuit. Electric current flows through the motor (which makes the motor's shaft spin) and through the LEDs (which light up). As the motor spins, it turns the propeller. The propeller blades push on the air as they move – and that makes the car move forward. The car will pick up speed, so you'll have to be ready to catch it!

Real-world inventions
Solar Impulse 2

The Solar Impulse 2 is an aeroplane that uses electricity in a similar way to your breadboard car. It has four powerful electric motors that turn propellers. The electricity to turn the motors is provided by solar panels across the wings, which generate power whenever sunlight hits them. The energy from the solar panels is stored in batteries, so the plane can even fly at night.

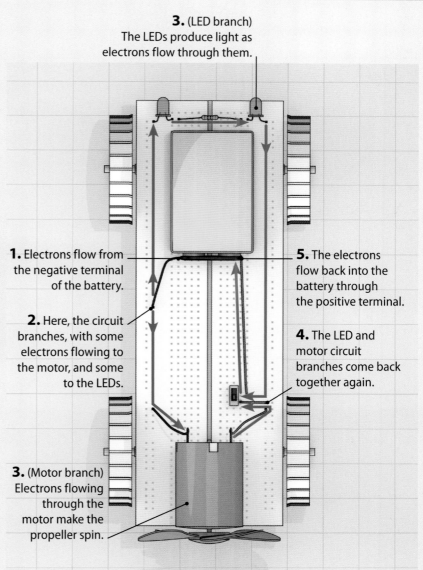

3. (LED branch) The LEDs produce light as electrons flow through them.

1. Electrons flow from the negative terminal of the battery.

2. Here, the circuit branches, with some electrons flowing to the motor, and some to the LEDs.

3. (Motor branch) Electrons flowing through the motor make the propeller spin.

5. The electrons flow back into the battery through the positive terminal.

4. The LED and motor circuit branches come back together again.

Remote-controlled snake

Remote controls allow you to make things happen
at a distance – like changing the channel on the TV or
steering a drone. In this project, you'll operate a snake
that slithers across the floor by remote control. It'll take
a bit of practice, but soon you will be making your snake
twist and turn as it whizzes along the floor.

Under each of the
snake's body segments
are two beads that act
as wheels.

The control wires send
instructions from the switches
on the remote control to the
motors at the snake's head.

You can use cable ties
or tape to bundle the
control wires together.

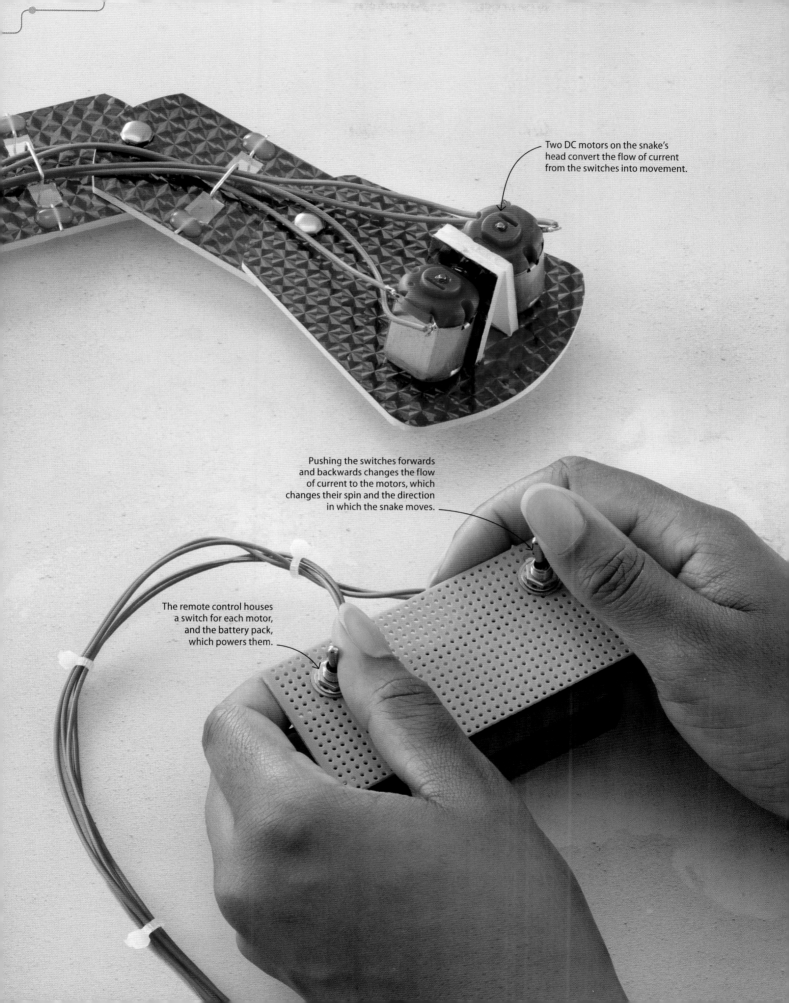

Two DC motors on the snake's head convert the flow of current from the switches into movement.

Pushing the switches forwards and backwards changes the flow of current to the motors, which changes their spin and the direction in which the snake moves.

The remote control houses a switch for each motor, and the battery pack, which powers them.

How to make a
Remote-controlled snake

The key to this project are DPDT switches, which allow current to flow in either direction or turn it off completely. When you join the snake's body segments, make sure they can swivel – otherwise the snake will not slither! You can stick decorative paper onto one side of the foam board to give your snake some colour.

Time
1 hour

Be aware
Requires utility knife, hot-glue gun, soldering iron, and drill use.

Difficulty
Hard

What you need

From the toolbox:

- Utility knife
- Cutting mat
- Bradawl
- Ruler
- Wire cutters
- Pliers
- Hot-glue gun
- Wire strippers
- Soldering iron and solder
- Scrap wood and clamps
- Drill
- 6 mm (¼ in) drill bit
- Double-sided foam tape

(2x) 3–12-volt motors

(1x) 9-volt battery pack

(1x) 9-volt battery

Jewellery wire 50 cm (20 in)

(2x) DPDT switches ON/OFF/ON

(7x) Paper fasteners 15 mm (⁹⁄₁₆ in)

(1x) Stripboard 10 cm x 5 cm (4 in x 2 in)

(12x) Spacer beads 5 mm (¹³⁄₆₄ in)

Black stranded wire 8 cm (3⅛ in)

Red stranded wire 6 m 16 cm (20 ft)

Roll of wrapping paper

(1x) A4 foam board

Templates

Trace the three shapes here, and use that as a template to cut the shapes out below.

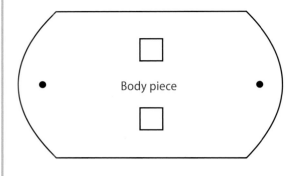

Body piece

You will need six body pieces, one head, and one tail.

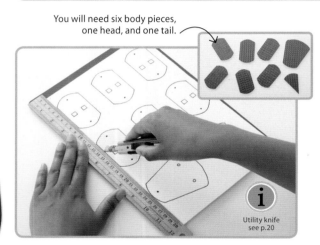

Utility knife see p.20

1 Stick your wrapping paper onto the foam board. Flip it over, and use the tracing paper to transfer the shapes above onto the foam board. Then use the utility knife to cut out the pieces.

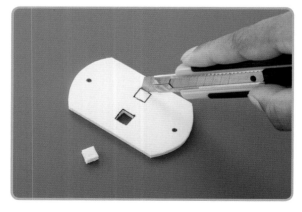

2 Using the utility knife, carefully cut out the squares in the body segments, and the two circles in the head piece.

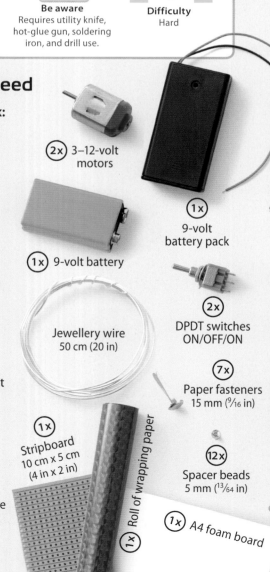

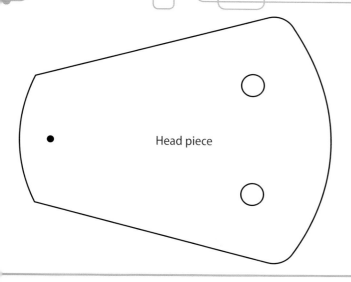

Head piece

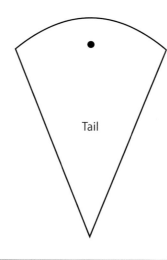

Tail

When you get to steps 4–6, refer to the shape below to bend your jewellery wire accurately to make the axles for the snake's wheels.

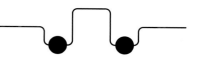

i

Using a bradawl see p.24

Using adhesive putty underneath the foam board will result in a cleaner hole, and will protect the surface.

3 Use the bradawl to poke holes through all the remaining markings on the six body segments and the head and tail.

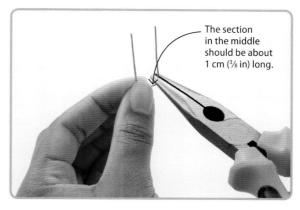

The section in the middle should be about 1 cm (³⁄₈ in) long.

4 Next, you will make the wheel axles for the snake. Cut an 8 cm (3¹⁄₈ in) piece of jewellery wire. Following the template above, use pliers to make two right-angle bends, so that the piece has a "U" shape.

Make sure the jewellery wire on each side of the "U" bend is level with the other.

5 Make two more right-angled bends in the wire, each about 1 cm (³⁄₈ in) away from either side of the existing bends. Now thread a bead onto the wire.

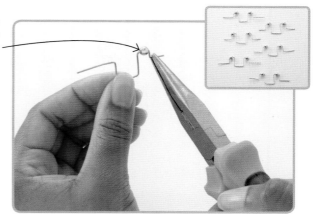

The beads will be the wheels for the body segments.

6 Put two more right-angled bends on the end of the wire so the bead cannot slip off. Repeat on the other side. Then, repeat steps 4–6 five more times, so you end up with six pieces of bent jewellery wire.

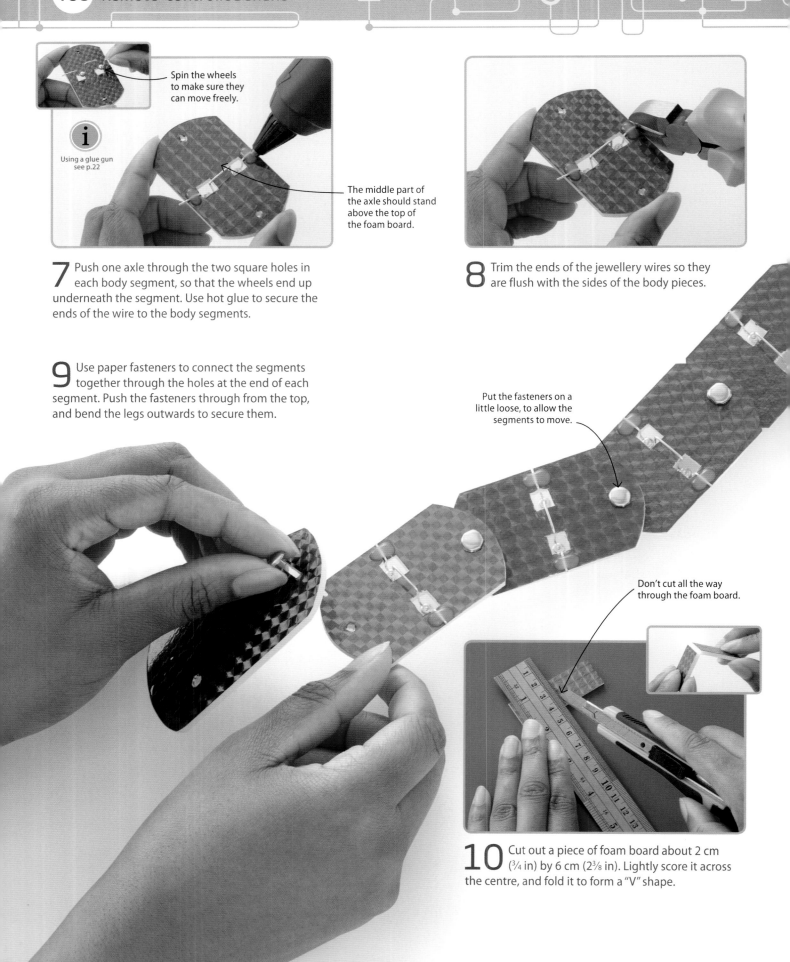

Spin the wheels to make sure they can move freely.

Using a glue gun see p.22

The middle part of the axle should stand above the top of the foam board.

7 Push one axle through the two square holes in each body segment, so that the wheels end up underneath the segment. Use hot glue to secure the ends of the wire to the body segments.

8 Trim the ends of the jewellery wires so they are flush with the sides of the body pieces.

9 Use paper fasteners to connect the segments together through the holes at the end of each segment. Push the fasteners through from the top, and bend the legs outwards to secure them.

Put the fasteners on a little loose, to allow the segments to move.

Don't cut all the way through the foam board.

10 Cut out a piece of foam board about 2 cm (¾ in) by 6 cm (2⅜ in). Lightly score it across the centre, and fold it to form a "V" shape.

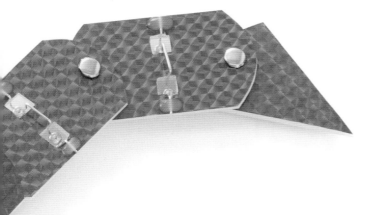

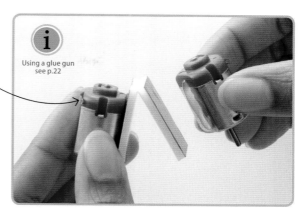

Make sure the
motors' terminals
face outwards.

Using a glue gun
see p.22

11 Use hot glue to attach the motors to either side of the "V" platform. Their shafts should face away from the scored edge, and the motors' bodies should align with the bottom edge of the platform.

12 Stand the motors on the snake's head, with the motors' shafts poking through the holes.

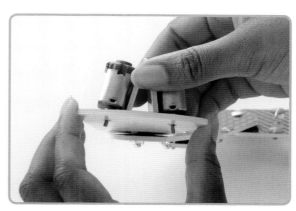

13 Glue the bottom of the platform to the top of the snake's head, making sure that the motor shafts are not touching the sides of the holes.

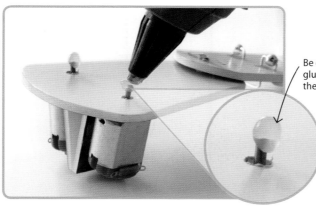

Be careful not to
glue the shafts to
the foam board.

14 Once the glue on the platform is dry, turn the snake over and put blobs of hot glue onto the ends of the motors' shafts.

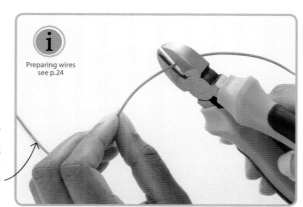

Preparing wires
see p.24

The longer
these wires are,
the further away
you can control
the snake from.

15 Cut four pieces of red stranded wire, each 1½ metres (5 ft) long. Strip the ends of all four wires.

16 Solder one end of each wire to each of the four motor terminals.

Soldering
see pp.25–26

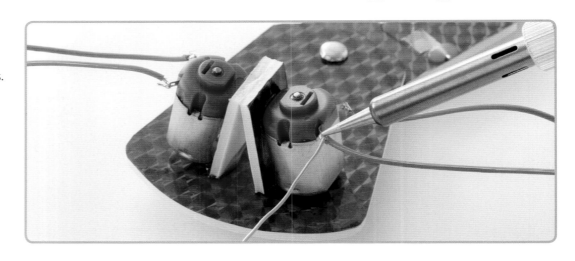

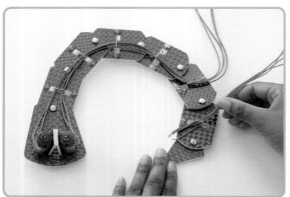

17 Thread all four long red wires through the middle of the axles where they project above the body segments.

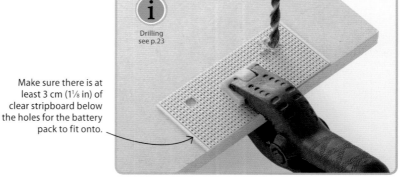

Drilling
see p.23

Make sure there is at least 3 cm (1⅛ in) of clear stripboard below the holes for the battery pack to fit onto.

18 Drill two 6 mm (¼ in) holes in the stripboard, each about 2 cm (¾ in) from the end and 1 cm (⅜ in) from the side. These holes will allow you to secure the DPDT switches.

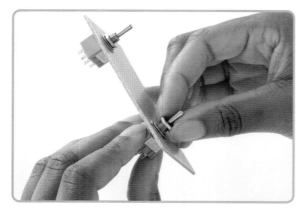

19 Place the DPDT switches into the holes in the stripboard, and screw on the washers and nuts from the other side.

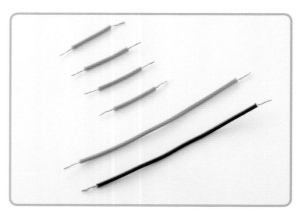

20 Next, cut four pieces of red stranded wire, each 2 cm (¾ in) long, and one black and one red wire each 8 cm (3⅛ in) long. Strip both ends of each wire.

21 Take the long red and black wires, and, following the key to the right, solder them to the middle connections on the DPDT switches. Use adhesive putty to hold the board in place on your work surface while you solder.

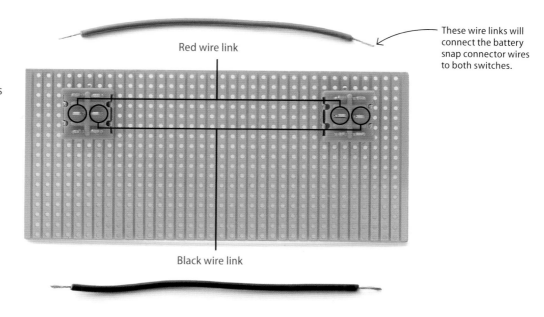

Red wire link

These wire links will connect the battery snap connector wires to both switches.

Black wire link

22 Strip the ends of the wires from the battery pack, and, following the key to the right, solder them to the righthand switch. You may need to trim the wires to size if they are too long.

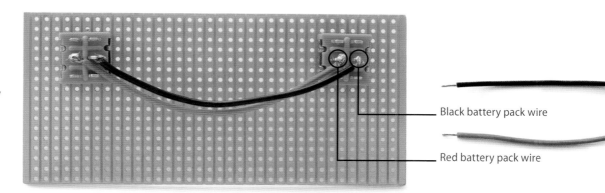

Black battery pack wire

Red battery pack wire

23 Next, following the key to the right, solder the four short red wire links to the switch terminals.

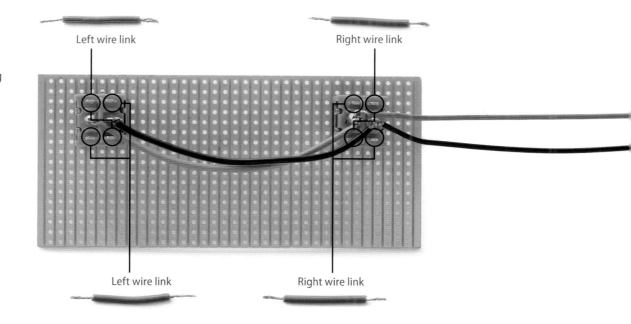

Left wire link

Right wire link

Left wire link

Right wire link

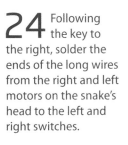

24 Following the key to the right, solder the ends of the long wires from the right and left motors on the snake's head to the left and right switches.

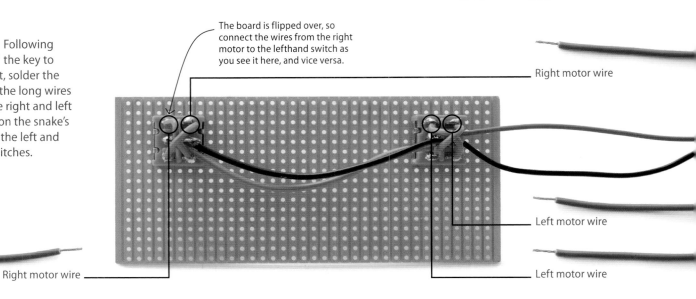

The board is flipped over, so connect the wires from the right motor to the lefthand switch as you see it here, and vice versa.

Right motor wire

Right motor wire

Left motor wire

Left motor wire

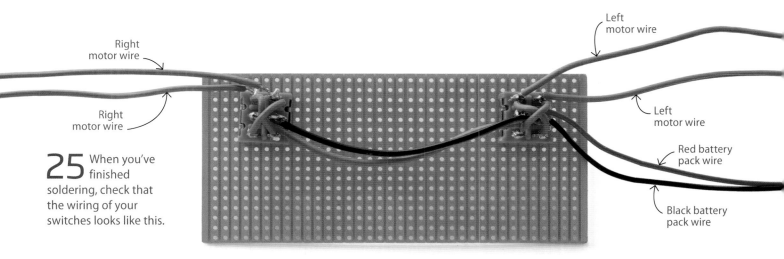

Right motor wire

Right motor wire

Left motor wire

Left motor wire

Red battery pack wire

Black battery pack wire

25 When you've finished soldering, check that the wiring of your switches looks like this.

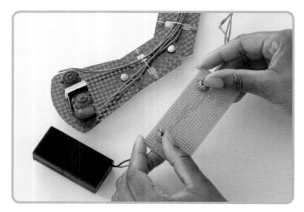

26 Place the 9v battery into the battery pack and push and pull the switches. If the motors don't spin, go back and check all of your connections.

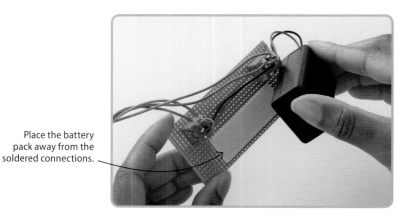

Place the battery pack away from the soldered connections.

27 Attach the battery pack to the underside of the stripboard using double-sided foam tape. Now flip both switches both ways, and watch the snake slither across the floor!

How it works

The motors' shafts can turn in either direction, depending on the direction of the current flowing through them. The blobs of glue on the motor shafts grip the floor, and when they spin, the friction between them and the floor helps the snake to to move.

The movement of the head is passed onto the body through the wheels and paper fasteners.

1. The switches on the remote control allow current to flow through each motor in either direction, or not at all.

When the switch is in neutral mode, no current flows to the motor.

2. The snake moves to the right when both motors spin to the right.

3. The snake moves forwards when the motor on the right spins to the left, and the motor on the left spins to the right. If you reverse this, the snake moves backwards.

4. The snake moves to the left when both motors spin to the left.

Real-world inventions
Wireless remote control

Most remotely controlled devices, like this drone, are not connected to their control by long wires. Instead, the control transmits coded radio signals that are received by the device. Different signals activate different motors or lights on the device. The batteries that power the device must be inside the device itself, rather than in the controller.

Circuit organ

In electronic music, each musical note is produced by an electric current oscillating (moving to-and-fro). The more rapidly the current oscillates, the more high-pitched the sound is. In this project, you'll make a circuit that produces electronic music, with switches that play different notes when you press them.

A series of resistors determines the pitch of the note the organ produces when a switch is pressed.

At the control centre of the organ is an integrated circuit (IC), which produces the oscillating electric currents.

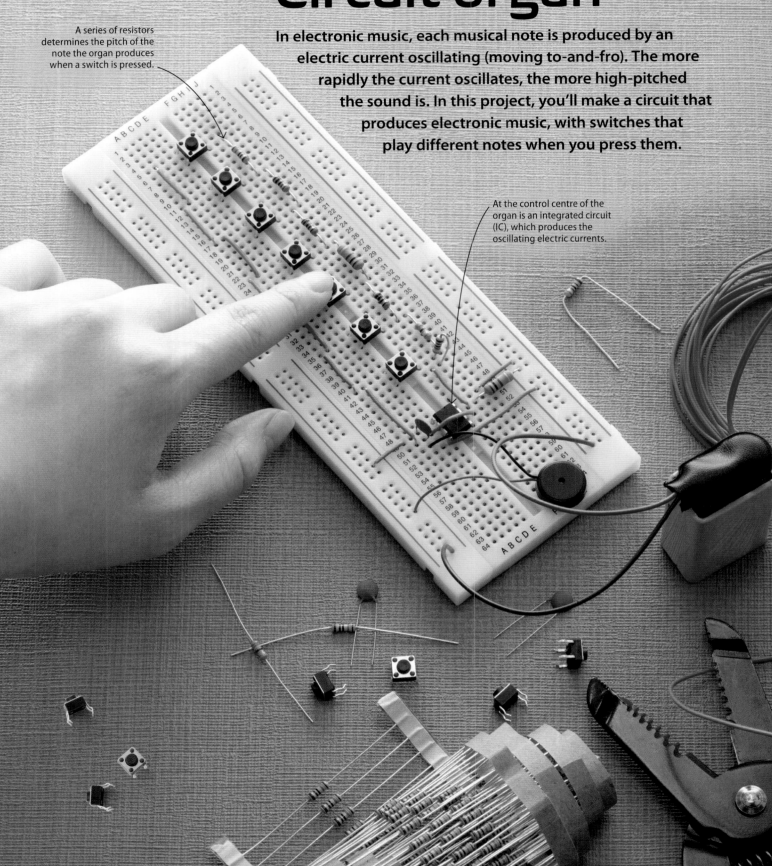

How to make a
Circuit organ

All the components of the organ are inserted into a breadboard. If the wires of your battery pack and sounder are stranded, you will need to tin them with the soldering iron before you begin.

Time	**Difficulty**
25 mins	Easy

What you need

From the toolbox

• Wire cutters

1x
9-volt battery

(7x)
Mini tactile button switches

1x
Battery snap connector

1x
100 nF capacitor

1x
Piezo sounder

(1x) **390 Ω resistor**

(1x) **620 Ω resistor**

(1x) **1.1 kΩ resistor**

(1x) **910 Ω resistor**

(1x) **1.3 kΩ resistor**

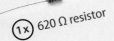

(2x) **1 kΩ resistors**

(1x) **6.2 kΩ resistor**

(1x)
555 timer IC

Solid-core wire
26 cm (10¼ in)

(1x) **840-pin breadboard**

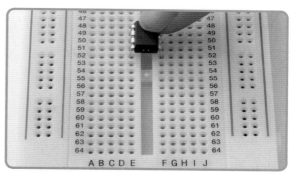

1 Push the 555 timer IC into the board with its rounded notch facing away from you, and with its corner legs in the holes for E49, F49, E52, and F52.

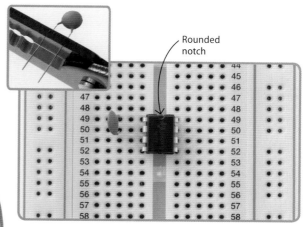

Rounded notch

2 Trim the legs of the capacitor, so that it won't stand too high on the board. Push the legs into holes C49 and C50 – it doesn't matter which way around it goes.

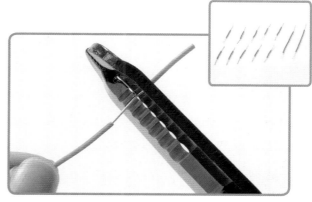

3 Cut 10 pieces of the solid-core wire, each about 2 cm (¾ in) long, and two pieces 3 cm (1⅛ in) long. Strip 6 mm (¼ in) off all of the ends, and bend the stripped parts down at right angles.

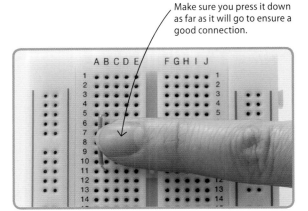

Make sure you press it down as far as it will go to ensure a good connection.

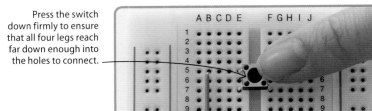

Press the switch down firmly to ensure that all four legs reach far down enough into the holes to connect.

4 Insert one of the short wires into holes B5 and B11 of the breadboard.

5 Push one of the button switches into the breadboard with its legs in holes E5, E7, F5, and F7.

6 Using the breadboard map to the right, insert the stripped and bent ends of the wires into their positions on the board.

7 Place the other button switches into the breadboard where shown. Make sure that each one is exactly three holes away from the one before.

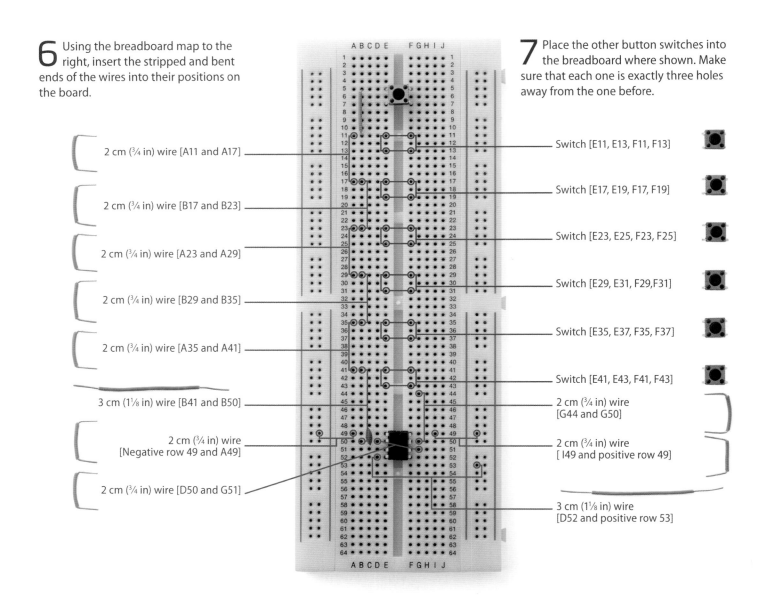

2 cm (¾ in) wire [A11 and A17]

2 cm (¾ in) wire [B17 and B23]

2 cm (¾ in) wire [A23 and A29]

2 cm (¾ in) wire [B29 and B35]

2 cm (¾ in) wire [A35 and A41]

3 cm (1⅛ in) wire [B41 and B50]

2 cm (¾ in) wire [Negative row 49 and A49]

2 cm (¾ in) wire [D50 and G51]

Switch [E11, E13, F11, F13]

Switch [E17, E19, F17, F19]

Switch [E23, E25, F23, F25]

Switch [E29, E31, F29, F31]

Switch [E35, E37, F35, F37]

Switch [E41, E43, F41, F43]

2 cm (¾ in) wire [G44 and G50]

2 cm (¾ in) wire [I49 and positive row 49]

3 cm (1⅛ in) wire [D52 and positive row 53]

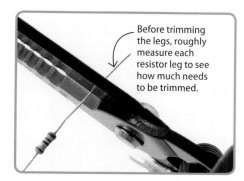

Before trimming the legs, roughly measure each resistor leg to see how much needs to be trimmed.

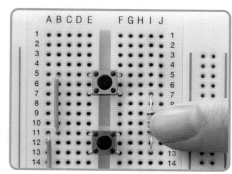

8 Next, you'll be pushing the resistors into the exact positions on the breadboard. You'll need to trim the legs to the correct length, but it's best to do this one-by-one, as you go along.

9 Remember to bend the ends of the resistors' legs at right angles, to make them easier to insert into the board, as you did with the lengths of solid-core wire.

10 Insert the 1.3 kΩ resistor into holes I1 and I7.

11 Using the breadboard map to the right, insert the trimmed and bent legs of the resistors into their positions on the board. It doesn't matter which way around the resistors go.

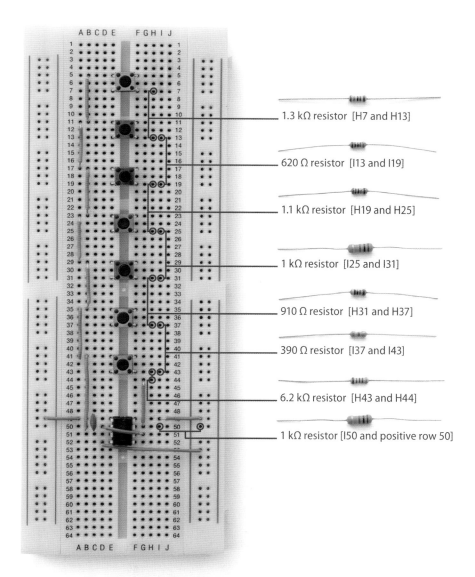

1.3 kΩ resistor [H7 and H13]

620 Ω resistor [I13 and I19]

1.1 kΩ resistor [H19 and H25]

1 kΩ resistor [I25 and I31]

910 Ω resistor [H31 and H37]

390 Ω resistor [I37 and I43]

6.2 kΩ resistor [H43 and H44]

1 kΩ resistor [I50 and positive row 50]

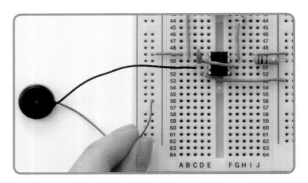

12 Push the black wire of the piezo sounder into C51 and the red wire into the negative side of row 56.

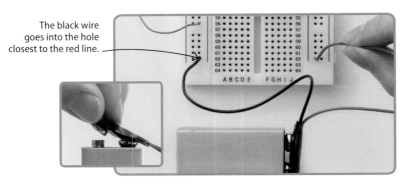

The black wire goes into the hole closest to the red line.

13 Snap the battery connector onto the battery, and push its black wire into negative row 62 on the left side, and the red wire into positive row 62 on the right side, as shown.

14 Your organ is now complete. Pressing the button switches will cause the sounder to make a sound. Each switch you press produces a different musical note.

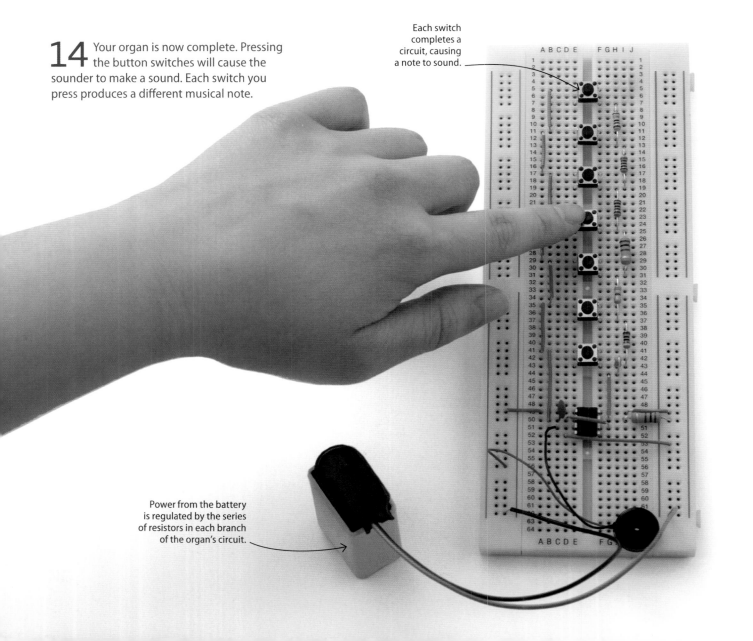

Each switch completes a circuit, causing a note to sound.

Power from the battery is regulated by the series of resistors in each branch of the organ's circuit.

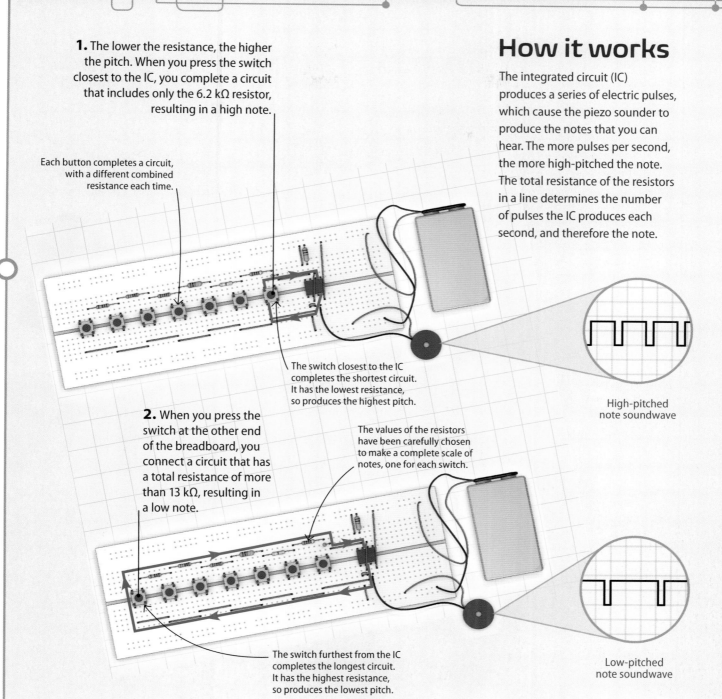

1. The lower the resistance, the higher the pitch. When you press the switch closest to the IC, you complete a circuit that includes only the 6.2 kΩ resistor, resulting in a high note.

Each button completes a circuit, with a different combined resistance each time.

The switch closest to the IC completes the shortest circuit. It has the lowest resistance, so produces the highest pitch.

2. When you press the switch at the other end of the breadboard, you connect a circuit that has a total resistance of more than 13 kΩ, resulting in a low note.

The values of the resistors have been carefully chosen to make a complete scale of notes, one for each switch.

The switch furthest from the IC completes the longest circuit. It has the highest resistance, so produces the lowest pitch.

How it works

The integrated circuit (IC) produces a series of electric pulses, which cause the piezo sounder to produce the notes that you can hear. The more pulses per second, the more high-pitched the note. The total resistance of the resistors in a line determines the number of pulses the IC produces each second, and therefore the note.

High-pitched note soundwave

Low-pitched note soundwave

Real-world inventions
Piano

Like your circuit organ, a piano produces different musical notes, from high- to low-pitched. A piano produces sound when strings are made to vibrate by hammers that strike them when you hit a key. The shorter, thinner strings make higher-pitched notes than the longer, thicker strings.

Bottle boat

Make some waves with this shipshape, propeller-powered boat! This boat uses batteries to drive two electric motors, which each spin a propeller. A propeller is a type of fan that turns rotational (spinning) motion into thrust, which allows your boat to go forward. Float your boat in the water, turn it on, and watch it go!

Flipping the switch allows electric current to flow through the boat's twin motors.

The boat's motors turn two screw propellers, which drive the boat through the water.

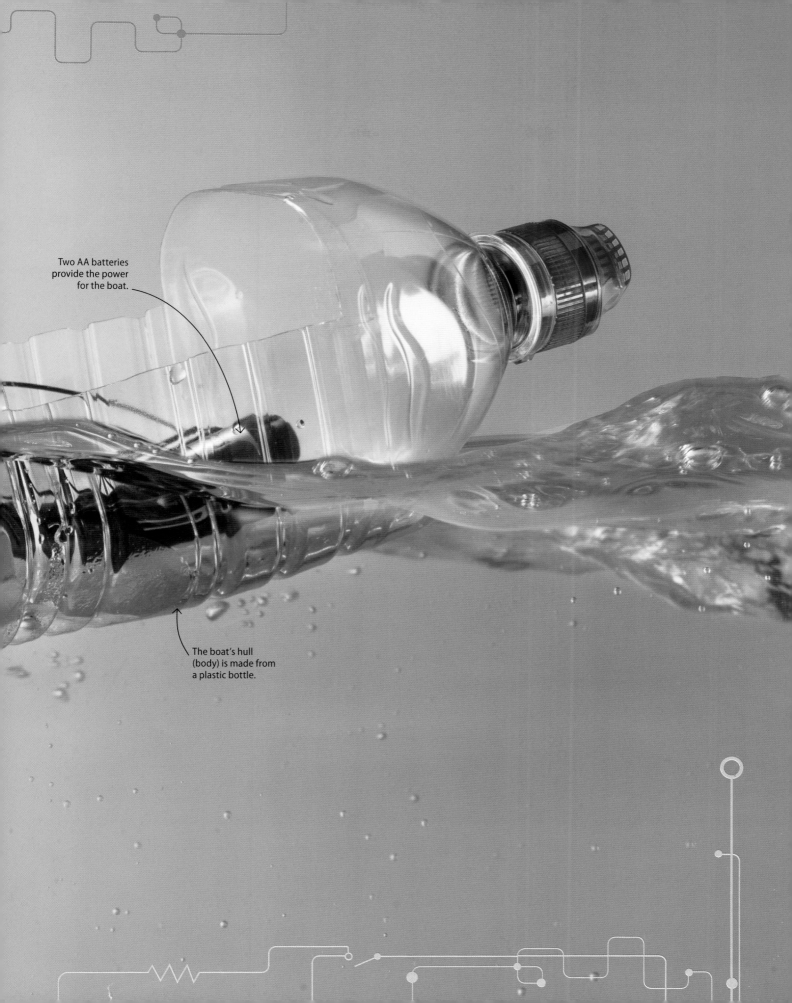

Two AA batteries provide the power for the boat.

The boat's hull (body) is made from a plastic bottle.

How to make a
Bottle boat

The tricky part of this project is making a platform at the stern (back) of the boat for the motors to sit on – and making sure the boat is watertight. The hard plastic tube can be bought from craft shops. Make sure that its diameter is more than that of the pen's ink tube.

Time
60 mins

Be aware
Requires utility knife, bradawl, hot-glue gun, and soldering iron use.

Difficulty
Medium

What you need

From the toolbox

- Utility knife
- Bradawl
- Cutting mat
- Hot-glue gun
- Ruler
- Wire cutters
- Wire strippers
- Soldering iron and solder
- Third-hand tool
- Double-sided foam tape

1x 3-volt battery pack

2x 6-volt motors

2x AA batteries

2x Metal propeller shafts

1x SPST switch

1x Battery snap connector

2x Small model boat screw propellers

Black stranded wire 20 cm (8 in)

1x Polystyrene board

1x Hard plastic tube

2x Ballpoint pens

Red stranded wire 20 cm (8 in)

1x Plastic bottle with straight sides

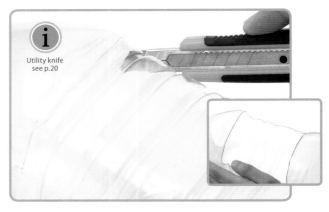

Utility knife see p.20

1 Use the utility knife to cut a large rectangle out of the middle of one side of the bottle. Be careful not to cut too far down on the sides.

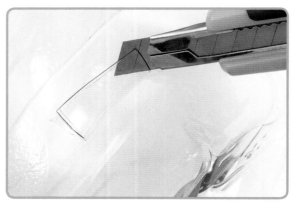

2 Near the base of the bottle, cut out a rectangle that is slightly smaller than the SPST switch and is in line with the middle of the larger hole.

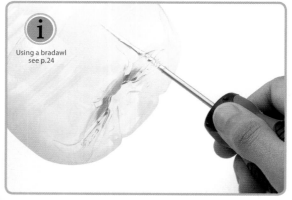

Using a bradawl see p.24

3 Use the bradawl to make two holes about halfway up the bottom of the bottle, on either side of the centre. Make the holes slightly larger than the diameter of the hard plastic tube.

4 Use the utility knife to cut two equal lengths of the hard plastic tube, about 1 cm (⅜ in) shorter than the metal propeller shafts.

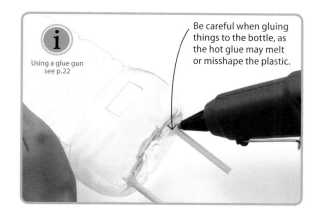

Be careful when gluing things to the bottle, as the hot glue may melt or misshape the plastic.

Using a glue gun see p.22

5 Push the plastic tubes into the holes in the bottom of the bottle, and hot-glue them into place. Make sure the tubes are both positioned downwards at an angle of about 30°.

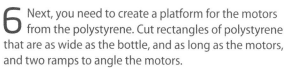

Cut as many rectangles as you need so that the motors can reach the holes in the bottom of the bottle.

6 Next, you need to create a platform for the motors from the polystyrene. Cut rectangles of polystyrene that are as wide as the bottle, and as long as the motors, and two ramps to angle the motors.

7 Hot-glue the rectangles together. Don't put the nozzle of the hot-glue gun close to the surface for too long as it could melt the polystyrene.

9 Now glue the two triangular ramps on either side of the top of the glued polystyrene rectangles.

Discard the pieces you don't need.

8 You may need to trim the polystyrene to fit snugly inside the bottle.

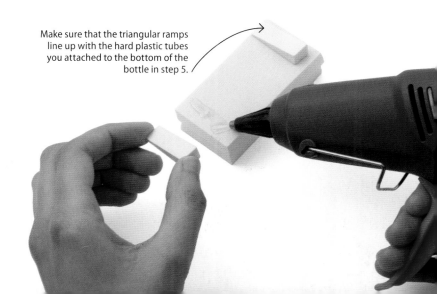

Make sure that the triangular ramps line up with the hard plastic tubes you attached to the bottom of the bottle in step 5.

10 Apply hot glue to the underside of the polystyrene platform and secure it in place at the base of the bottle.

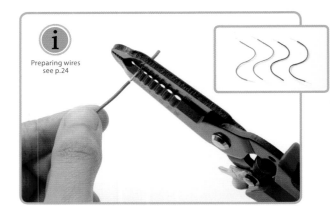

Preparing wires
see p.24

11 Cut, strip, and tin two red wires and two black wires approximately 10 cm (4 in) long. Strip and tin the wires on the battery snap connector, too.

Soldering
see pp.25–26

12 Solder one black wire to one of the terminals of each of the DC motors. Then take the two red wires and solder them to the other terminal on each motor.

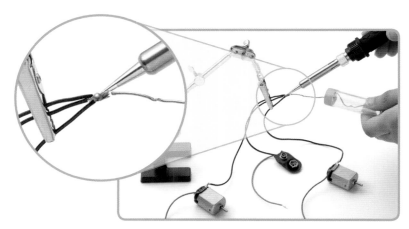

13 Solder the black wires from the motors and the black wire from the battery snap connector together to create a three-way junction.

14 Place the motors, wires, and battery snap connector into the hull of the boat. Feed the red wires through the smaller rectangle that you cut in step 2 for the SPST switch.

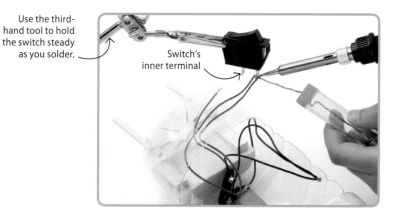

Use the third-hand tool to hold the switch steady as you solder.

Switch's inner terminal

15 Solder the red wires from the motors to the outer SPST switch terminal, creating a two-way junction. Then solder the red wire from the battery snap connector to the inner switch terminal.

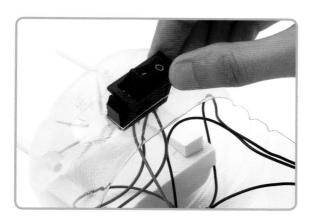

16 Slot the SPST switch into the hole, making sure that it sits snugly and won't fall out. Ensure that the wires don't get caught between the switch and the switch's slot.

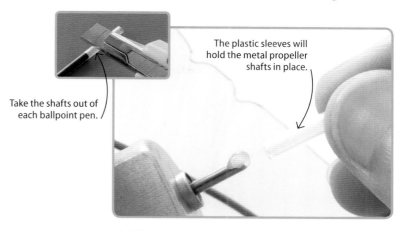

The plastic sleeves will hold the metal propeller shafts in place.

Take the shafts out of each ballpoint pen.

17 Now, take the shafts out of the ballpoint pens. Cut 1 cm (⅜ in) off the ends of the shafts, to create plastic sleeves. Use a little hot glue to secure a sleeve onto each motor shaft.

18 Use a small strip of double-sided foam tape to stick each motor down onto one of the polystyrene ramps.

You can use hot glue to fix the motors in place if you wish.

The join between the propeller and shaft should be tight.

The polystyrene base will be stuck to the boat's base.

19 Push the model boat propellers onto the two metal shafts. Pass the shafts through the plastic tubes and push them firmly into the open end of each of the plastic sleeves.

20 Cut out a rectangular piece of polystyrene large enough for your battery pack to sit on. Use the battery pack as a guide.

21 Use hot glue to stick the battery pack to the polystyrene, then connect the battery snap connector to the battery holder.

How it works

The type of propellers on your boat has a huge effect on how well it moves itself forward in water. The propellers on your boat are called screw propellers: the curve of the propeller blades is similar to a screw's thread.

1. When you press the boat's switch, the circuit is complete.

The straight sides of the bottle stop it from rolling in the water.

2. Electricity flows through the motors, and the motors' torque (turning force) is transferred to the propellers.

The bottle's narrow shape helps it cut through the water better by reducing hydrodynamic drag on the boat. Hydrodynamics is the the study of fluids in motion, and drag is the force acting upon the boat that resists its movement.

The current splits here, which means the motors are wired in parallel. As a result, they both get the same amount of current, which is important for the boat to maintain a forward direction.

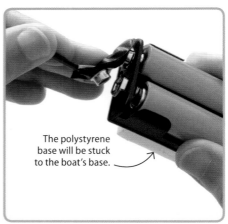

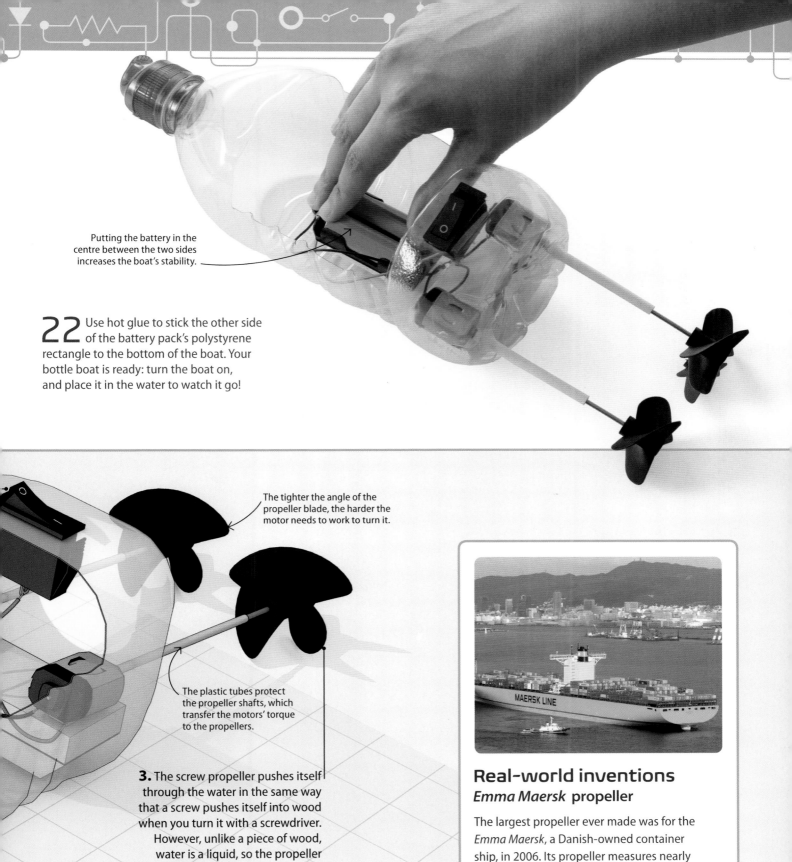

Putting the battery in the centre between the two sides increases the boat's stability.

22 Use hot glue to stick the other side of the battery pack's polystyrene rectangle to the bottom of the boat. Your bottle boat is ready: turn the boat on, and place it in the water to watch it go!

The tighter the angle of the propeller blade, the harder the motor needs to work to turn it.

The plastic tubes protect the propeller shafts, which transfer the motors' torque to the propellers.

3. The screw propeller pushes itself through the water in the same way that a screw pushes itself into wood when you turn it with a screwdriver. However, unlike a piece of wood, water is a liquid, so the propeller pushes some water backwards as the boat moves forward.

Real-world inventions
Emma Maersk propeller

The largest propeller ever made was for the *Emma Maersk*, a Danish-owned container ship, in 2006. Its propeller measures nearly 10 m (32 ft) in diameter – the height of three adult elephants! It's made of bronze and has a mass of more than 125 tonnes.

Pipe stereo

Portable stereo speakers can be quite expensive to buy, but you can assemble your own for a fraction of the cost. In this project, the audio signal from a smartphone is passed through a circuit called an amplifier, which makes the signal powerful enough to be heard through two speakers.

A smartphone's computer produces an audio signal when it plays music or videos.

The body of this stereo unit is made of sections of plastic pipe from a hardware store.

Each speaker has a paper cone that vibrates to produce sound.

How to make a
Pipe stereo

At the heart of this build is a ready-made electronic circuit called an amplifier. The one you'll use runs on five volts supplied by a USB cable, which you need to plug into a USB socket (such as on a computer, or the type used to charge a smartphone). There's lots of cutting, stripping, and soldering, so take your time.

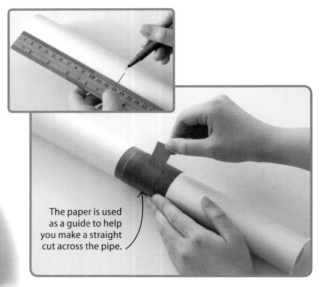

Time 60 mins	**Be aware** Requires hacksaw, soldering iron, hot-glue gun, and mains electricity use.	**Difficulty** Hard

What you need

From the toolbox:

- Marker
- Ruler
- Tape
- Scrap wood
- Hacksaw
- Sandpaper
- Wire cutters
- Wire strippers
- Third-hand tool
- Soldering iron and solder
- Multimeter
- 8 mm (⁵⁄₁₆ in) drill bit
- Drill
- Hot-glue gun

(1x) Stereo minijack-to-minijack cable 50 cm (19¾ in)

(1x) PAM8403 5V amplifier module board

(2x) 90° PVC pipe elbows 40 mm (1½ in)

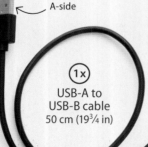

A-side

(1x) USB-A to USB-B cable 50 cm (19¾ in)

B-side

Red stranded wire 50 cm (19¾ in)

Black stranded wire 50 cm (19¾ in)

(1x) Paper 15 cm x 4 cm (5⅞ in x 1½ in)

(1x) PVC pipe 40 mm (1½ in)

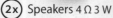

(2x) Speakers 4 Ω 3 W

The paper is used as a guide to help you make a straight cut across the pipe.

1 Make a mark 13 cm (5⅛ in) in from one end of the PVC pipe. Wrap a piece of paper around the pipe so that one edge of the paper lies at the mark. Tape the paper down.

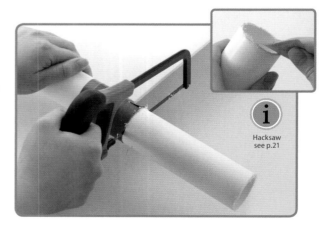

(i) Hacksaw see p.21

2 With the length of pipe over the edge of a table or workbench, saw through the PVC pipe, using the edge of the paper as a guide. Treat the pipe's edges with sandpaper to make them smooth.

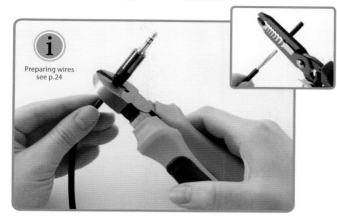

3 Cut and discard one minijack from the minijack-to-minijack cable. Strip away about 2½ cm (1 in) of the outer insulation, being careful not to cut through the internal wires.

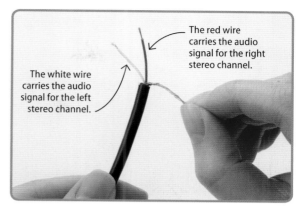

The red wire carries the audio signal for the right stereo channel.

The white wire carries the audio signal for the left stereo channel.

4 Separate the red and white internal wires, and strip about 1 cm (⅜ in) of insulation from the ends. Twist the strands of the all-copper wire together.

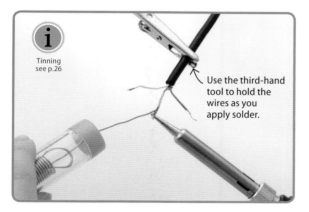

Tinning see p.26

Use the third-hand tool to hold the wires as you apply solder.

5 Tin the twisted ends of each of the three wires with solder. This will make it easier to solder them later. The copper wire is the "ground" wire – just tin the tip of this wire.

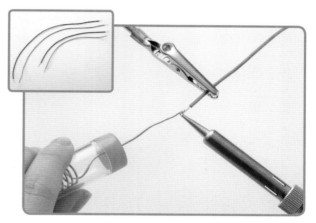

6 From the red and black stranded wire, cut lengths of wire about 30 cm (12 in) long. Next, cut some more lengths of about 20 cm (8 in) long. Strip about 1 cm (⅜ in) of insulation off the ends, and tin one end of each wire.

7 Tin the terminals of both speakers. This will make it easier to connect wires to them later.

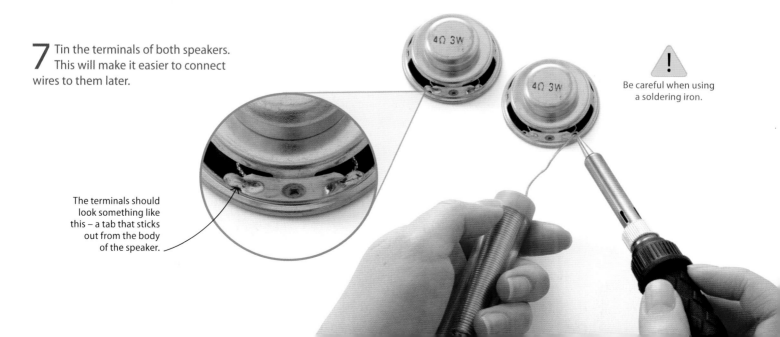

The terminals should look something like this – a tab that sticks out from the body of the speaker.

4Ω 3W

4Ω 3W

⚠ Be careful when using a soldering iron.

Preparing wires see p.24

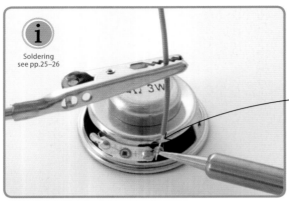

Soldering
see pp.25–26

Solder the wires across the terminals, so they reach towards the back of the speaker.

8 Solder the tinned ends of the shorter wires to the terminals of one speaker – red to the positive (marked "+") and black to the negative (marked "–"). Repeat with the longer wires on the other speaker.

9 Cut off the B-side of the USB lead, then strip the outer insulation from the end. Separate out the wires inside, and cut away everything except the four coloured wires.

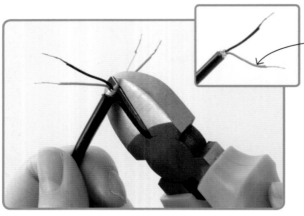

The positive and negative leads are usually the red and black wires.

10 Plug the USB cable into a USB socket and test the four wires with a multimeter, to find out which are the positive and negative wires. Strip and tin their ends, and cut off the other two wires.

Using a multimeter
see pp.28–29

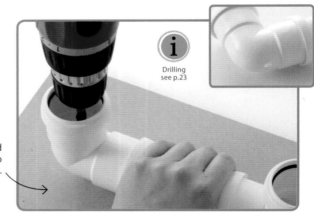

Drilling
see p.23

Use scrap wood when drilling to protect the surface.

11 Push the two elbow fittings onto the straight piece of pipe, and drill a hole about 8 mm (5/16 in) in diameter into the centre of the back of each elbow fitting.

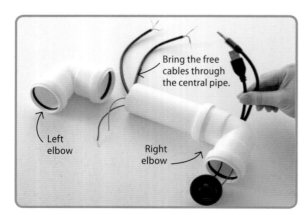

Bring the free cables through the central pipe.

Left elbow

Right elbow

12 Remove the left elbow, and fit the speaker with the longer wires into the right elbow. Feed the trimmed ends of the USB and minijack cables through the hole in the right elbow.

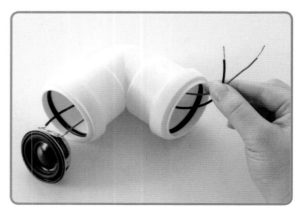

13 Fit the speaker with the shorter wires into the left elbow, and bring the red and black wires through the open end of the PVC elbow.

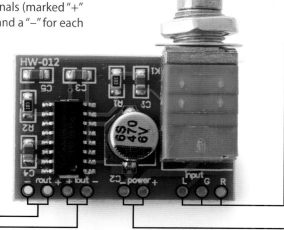

14 Locate the terminals on the amplifier circuit board. You should find three input terminals (labelled "L", "G", and "R"), two power terminals (marked "+" and "−"), and four output terminals (a "+" and a "−" for each of the right and left stereo channels).

The "Rout" positive and negative terminals are where the wires from the speaker on the right will be soldered.

The "Lout" positive and negative terminals are where the wires from the speaker on the left will be soldered.

The minijack lead wires will be soldered into the input terminals. The terminals are labelled "L" for left, "R" for right, and "G" for ground.

The USB wires will be soldered into the "+" and "-" power terminals.

15 Feed the right speaker's red wire through the positive "Rout" terminal, and the black wire through the negative "Rout" terminal. Repeat for the left speaker, feeding the wires through the "Lout" terminals.

You can trim the extra wire from the board after soldering.

16 Turn over the circuit board and hold it in place with the third-hand tool. Solder the speaker wires you have just connected. Make sure the bare part of the wires that are next to each other do not touch.

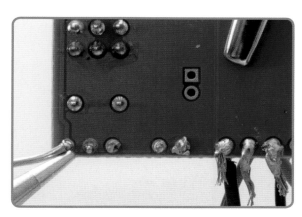

17 Use solder to tin the input and power terminals underneath the amplifier circuit board.

Again, make sure wires next to each other don't touch.

18 Solder the red wire of the minijack cable to the right ("R") input terminal, the white wire to the left ("L") input terminal, and the twisted copper wire to the ground ("G") terminal.

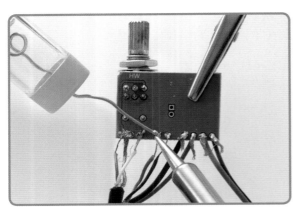

19 Solder the ends of the wires in the USB cable to the power terminals. Attach the positive (red) wire to the positive terminal ("+") and the negative (black) wire to the negative terminal ("−").

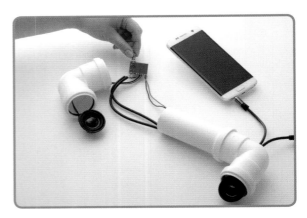

20 To test the stereo, plug the USB cable into a power source, and plug the minijack into a smartphone playing music. Turn the amplifier volume knob. If you can't hear anything, check the connections.

21 Carefully fix the speakers into the elbow fittings with hot glue. In each case, make sure you don't get any glue on the speaker's paper cone.

The volume knob may switch off the amplifier with a click when you turn it all the way down.

22 Remove the nut from the volume knob on the circuit board, then push the knob through the hole in the left elbow fitting. Screw the nut back on to secure the circuit board in place. Push all of the pipes together, and play your music!

The USB will draw power from any USB socket, such as on a computer, or a USB-to-mains charger.

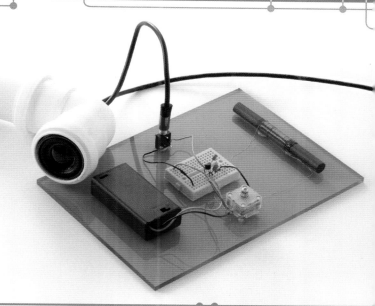

Cool sounds!

If you have completed the radio project in this book (see pp.84–89), you can plug the minijack from your pipe stereo into the headphone socket of the radio circuit. The sounds from the radio will play loud and clear through the pipe stereo.

How it works

Audio signals produced at the headphone jack of a smartphone are not strong enough to be heard through loudspeakers. The amplifier circuit uses current supplied by the USB cable to boost the power of the audio signals.

1. The headphone jack of the smartphone produces the audio signal, which is passed by the minijack cable to the stereo's amplifier.

2. The amplifier circuit increases the power of the audio signals, and sends them to both speakers.

3. A paper cone in each loudspeaker is connected to a coil of wire that sits between the poles of a magnet.

4. Electric current produced by the amplified audio signals passes through the coil.

5. The force between the coil and the magnet causes the paper cone to vibrate, creating sound waves.

Real world inventions
Very loud speakers

Huge, powerful speakers are used at concerts to produce sound waves powerful enough for all the audience to hear the music. These are so powerful that standing too close to them can damage your hearing!

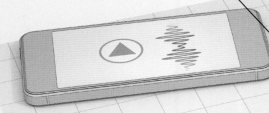

The plastic box contains a breadboard circuit that detects when the coil comes close to a ferrous metal.

The speaker produces a sound that changes pitch when the coil is near to a ferrous material.

The coil of copper wire produces a powerful magnetic field when electric current from the battery is running through it.

Steel is made mostly of iron, so your sensor will detect steel nails, nuts, and bolts.

Ferrous metal sensor

In this project, you'll build a sensor that can identify objects made of ferrous materials – materials that contain iron – even if they are hidden from view. It works in a similar way to metal detectors, as both inventions use a magnetic field produced by a coil of wire. Your sensor produces a high-pitched sound that changes pitch whenever the coil is close to a ferrous material.

How to make a
Ferrous metal sensor

It's okay if you can't find any old CDs – try to find something sturdy with the same dimensions of 12 cm (4¾ in) in diameter. The electronic circuit is housed inside a hard plastic box. Boxes of this kind are popular with makers, as they protect components from damage.

Time	Be aware	Difficulty
60 mins	Requires hot-glue gun, drill, and soldering iron use.	Hard

What you need

From the toolbox:

- Hot-glue gun
- Ruler
- Wire cutters
- Sandpaper
- Double-sided foam tape
- Marker
- Scrap wood and clamps
- Drill
- 5 mm (¹³⁄₆₄ in) drill bit
- Wire strippers
- Soldering iron
- Solder
- Third-hand tool
- Screwdriver

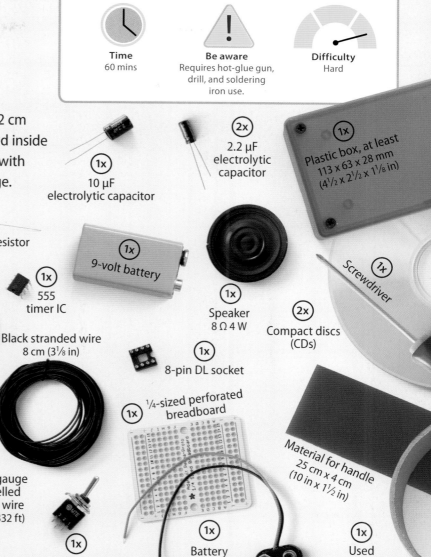

(1x) 10 µF electrolytic capacitor

(2x) 2.2 µF electrolytic capacitor

(1x) Plastic box, at least 113 x 63 x 28 mm (4½ x 2½ x 1⅛ in)

(1x) 47 kΩ resistor

(1x) 555 timer IC

(1x) 9-volt battery

(1x) Speaker 8 Ω 4 W

(2x) Compact discs (CDs)

(1x) Screwdriver

Red stranded wire 31 cm (12¼ in)

Black stranded wire 8 cm (3⅛ in)

(1x) 8-pin DL socket

(1x) ¼-sized perforated breadboard

32–36-gauge enamelled copper wire 101 m (332 ft)

Material for handle 25 cm x 4 cm (10 in x 1½ in)

(1x) SPDT switch

(1x) Battery snap connector

(1x) Used tape roll

i Using a glue gun see p.22

1 Use hot glue to attach the used tape roll to the centre of one of the CDs.

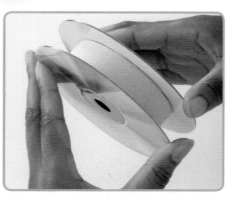

2 Glue the second CD to the other side of the used tape roll.

3 Use the hot-glue gun to secure one end of the copper wire where the used tape roll and CD meet, leaving about 20 cm (8 in) free at the end.

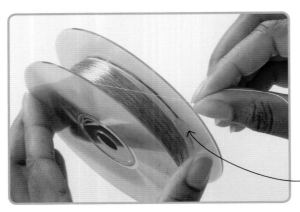

Make sure you don't cover the free end from step 3 as you wind the coil.

4 Wind about 400 turns of the copper wire around the used tape roll. Then cut the wire, leaving about 20 cm (8 in) free at the end.

5 Leaving about 20 cm (8 in) free at the end, use hot glue to secure the copper wire beside the other end of the wire. You should now have two free lengths of wire of 20 cm (8 in).

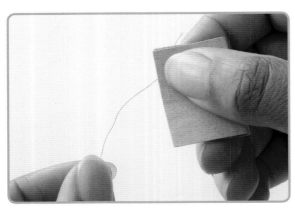

6 Scrape away about 2 cm (¾ in) of the coating from each end of the copper wire using sandpaper.

Make sure the free ends of wire face away from the longer end of the handle.

7 Now, attach your handle across the middle of one of the CDs with double-sided tape. Align the handle with the edge of the CD as best you can.

8 Open the plastic box – you may have to use a screwdriver to loosen the screws, or simply pull off a cover. Following the guide below, use a pen to mark where the switch, speaker wires, and wires from the coil will go.

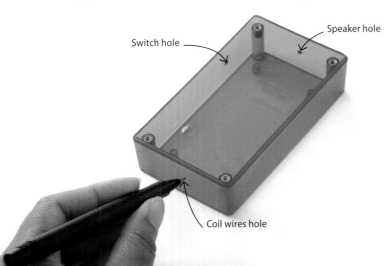

Switch hole

Speaker hole

Coil wires hole

ⓘ Drilling see p.23

9 Select a drill bit suitable for plastic – ask an adult if you're not sure – and drill three 5 mm (¹³⁄₆₄ in) holes through each of the markings on the plastic box.

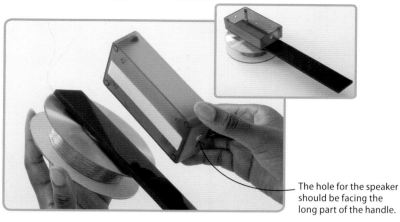
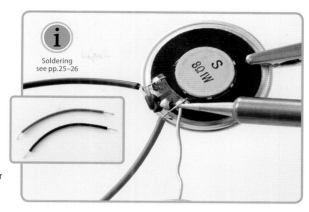

The hole for the speaker should be facing the long part of the handle.

10 Using double-sided foam tape, attach the plastic box to the handle. Align the bottom of the box with the edge of the handle.

11 Cut a black and a red wire, each 8 cm (3⅛ in) long. Strip the ends, and tin one end of each wire. Solder the black wire to the negative terminal of the speaker and the red wire to the positive terminal.

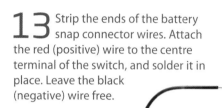

Soldering see pp.25–26

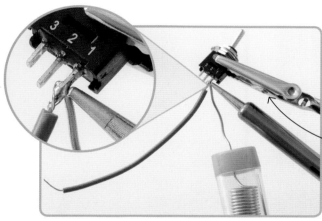

Use the third-hand tool to hold the switch while you solder.

13 Strip the ends of the battery snap connector wires. Attach the red (positive) wire to the centre terminal of the switch, and solder it in place. Leave the black (negative) wire free.

Hold the switch in the third-hand tool to keep it in place as you solder.

12 Cut a red wire 8 cm (3⅛) long and strip the ends. Feed one end through one of the outer terminals of the switch, twist it, and then secure it with solder.

These short wire links will form crucial connections in the circuit.

14 Cut four red wires: two 3 cm (1⅛ in) long, one 4 cm (1½ in) long, and one 5 cm (2 in) long. Strip and twist both ends of each wire, and bend the stripped ends at right angles.

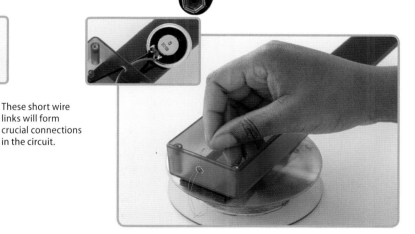

15 Feed the speaker wires through the hole at the top of the plastic box. Then feed the free ends of the coil through the hole on the opposite side.

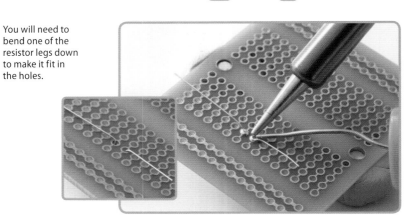

You will need to bend one of the resistor legs down to make it fit in the holes.

16 Push the legs of the 47 kΩ resistor through holes 8B and 9B on the breadboard, making sure the resistor sits on the top surface of the board.

17 Turn over the board and bend the resistor legs flat to hold it in place. Use a small amount of solder to secure the resistor, then trim the resistor legs with wire cutters.

18 Following the breadboard map below, push the 8-pin socket and the wire links into the board from the top. Solder them in place underneath the board, and cut away the excess wire. You can use adhesive putty to hold the board in place on your work surface while you solder.

Make sure the notch in the socket is facing this way when you solder it to the board.

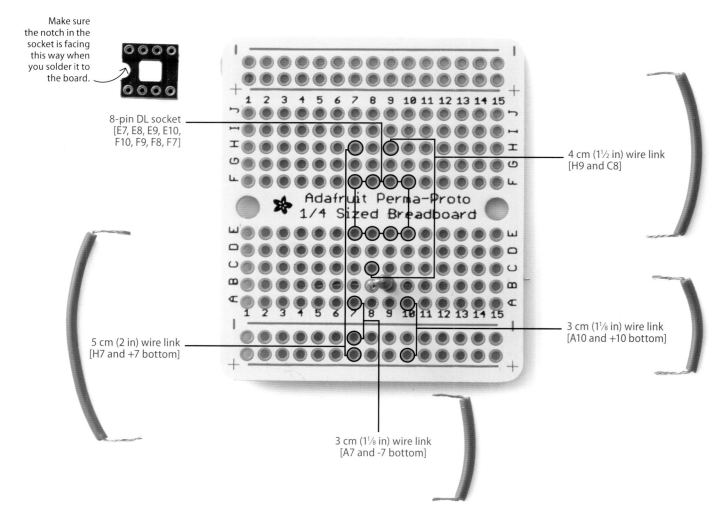

8-pin DL socket [E7, E8, E9, E10, F10, F9, F8, F7]

4 cm (1½ in) wire link [H9 and C8]

5 cm (2 in) wire link [H7 and +7 bottom]

3 cm (1⅛ in) wire link [A10 and +10 bottom]

3 cm (1⅛ in) wire link [A7 and -7 bottom]

19 Connect the other components and wires, as shown on the breadboard map below. Again, solder the wires and legs underneath the board, and cut off any excess. It is important that you feed the wires from the coil and the speaker through their holes before you solder them.

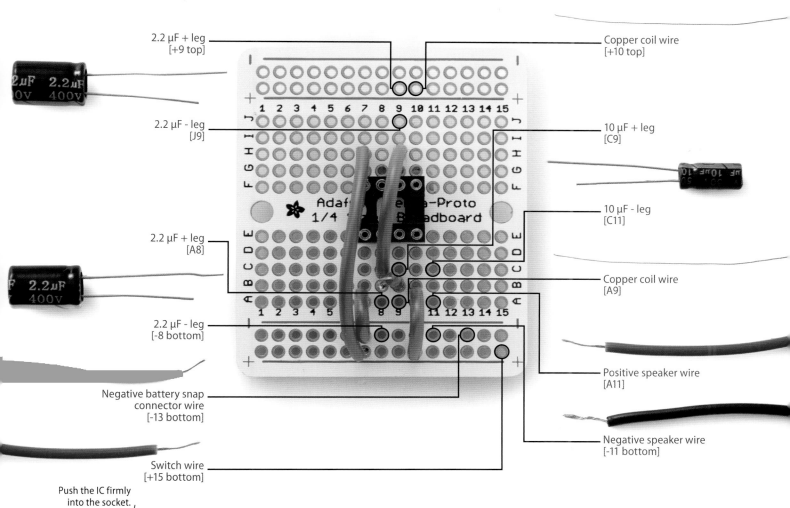

2.2 µF + leg [+9 top]

Copper coil wire [+10 top]

2.2 µF - leg [J9]

10 µF + leg [C9]

10 µF - leg [C11]

2.2 µF + leg [A8]

Copper coil wire [A9]

2.2 µF - leg [-8 bottom]

Positive speaker wire [A11]

Negative battery snap connector wire [-13 bottom]

Negative speaker wire [-11 bottom]

Switch wire [+15 bottom]

Push the IC firmly into the socket.

20 Plug the 555 IC timer into the 8-pin socket when you have finished soldering. The small notch on the 555 IC timer should align with the notch in the 8-pin DL socket.

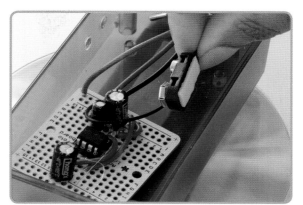

21 Stick a small piece of double-sided foam tape to the back of the battery snap connector, and stick it into the inside of the plastic box.

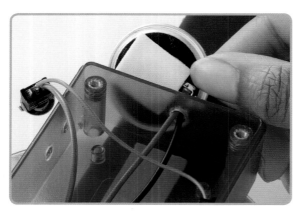

22 Use a small piece of double-sided foam tape to attach the back of the speaker to the outside of the plastic box, near the hole through which the speaker's wires pass.

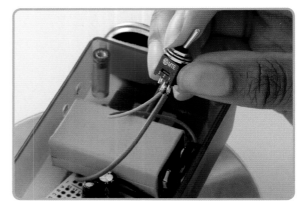

23 Connect the battery to the battery snap connector, and flip the switch. You should hear a high-pitched sound. If there is no sound, flip the switch off and go back and check the connections.

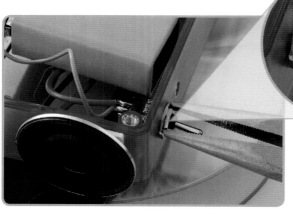

25 Replace the lid of the enclosure. Make sure the switch is turned on. Your ferrous metal sensor is ready for you to find things to test!

24 Unscrew the nut from the switch, and push the switch through the remaining hole in the plastic box from the inside out. Secure the nut on the other side with pliers.

The sound will change pitch whenever the coil is close to a ferrous metal.

How it works

When your ferrous metal sensor comes close to a material containing iron, it creates a magnetic field within that material. The interaction between magnetic fields in the sensor and the iron material causes a change of current in the ferrous metal sensor's coil.

1. The integrated circuit (IC) produces hundreds of electric pulses every second, which cause the speaker to produce the high-pitched sound.

2. When electric current is flowing through it, the coil of your metal detector produces a powerful electromagnetic field.

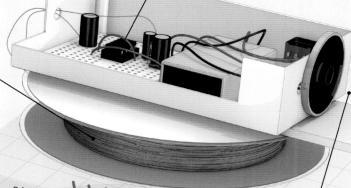

Primary magnetic field

3. The primary magnetic field of the coil creates, or induces, a secondary magnetic field inside any nearby ferrous materials.

Secondary magnetic field

5. The change in current affects the rate at which the IC produces the electric pulses – and that is why the sound the speaker produces changes pitch.

4. The secondary field interacts with the coil's primary magnetic field, changing the amount of current flowing through the coil.

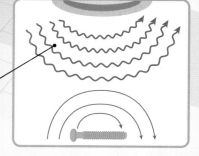

Real-world inventions
Metal detector

Treasure hunters use metal detectors to find old coins and other metallic artefacts buried underground. Their detectors have two coils. One produces a magnetic field that creates an electric current in any nearby metal. That current produces a magnetic field, which the second coil detects.

Automatic night light

The gentle glow of a night light in a hallway or in your bedroom can help you see a little better in the dark. The night light you'll make in this project uses a component called a photoresistor. The photoresistor automatically turns on a strip of LED lights at night time, and turns them off again in the morning.

You can change the design of your night light by changing the printed design on the front (known as a decal).

We've chosen space decals that look nice on the wall during the day.

The photoresistor sits on the front surface of the night light.

The night light must be plugged into the mains electricity to work.

The circuit that controls the LED strip is hidden behind the decal.

The LED strip is wrapped around the night light but hidden behind the decal, so that it casts a gentle glow on the wall.

How to make an
Automatic night light

You will need a cuttable LED strip to build this night light. LED strips can come in two, three, or four colours – any will work for this project. To make your decal, print a picture of your favourite design and cut it to the same size as your plywood disc.

Time	Be aware	Difficulty
1 hour	Requires drill, hot-glue gun, soldering iron, and mains electricity use.	Hard

What you need

From the toolbox:

- Scrap wood and clamps
- Drill
- 5 mm ($^{13}/_{64}$ in) drill bit
- 8 mm ($^5/_{16}$ in) drill bit
- Hot-glue gun
- Scissors
- Third-hand tool
- Soldering iron and solder
- Wire cutters
- Wire strippers
- Double-sided tape
- Adhesive putty

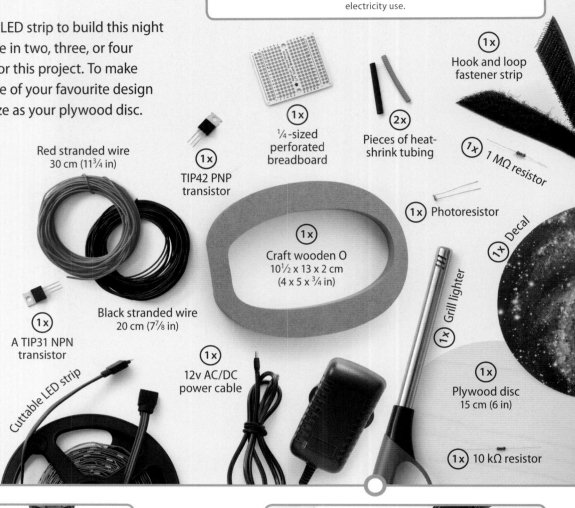

Red stranded wire 30 cm (11¾ in)

1x TIP42 PNP transistor

1x ¼-sized perforated breadboard

2x Pieces of heat-shrink tubing

1x Hook and loop fastener strip

1x 1 MΩ resistor

1x Photoresistor

1x Decal

1x Craft wooden O 10½ x 13 x 2 cm (4 x 5 x ¾ in)

Grill lighter

1x A TIP31 NPN transistor

Black stranded wire 20 cm (7⅞ in)

Cuttable LED strip

1x 12v AC/DC power cable

1x Plywood disc 15 cm (6 in)

1x 10 kΩ resistor

Drilling see p.23

1 Carefully drill a 5 mm ($^{13}/_{64}$ in) hole halfway through the wooden O. This hole is for hanging the night light on a nail or a hook. Then drill an 8 mm ($^5/_{16}$ in) hole through the opposite end.

Using a glue gun see p.22

2 Spread a little hot glue on one of the flat sides of the wooden O – the side that doesn't have the hole you drilled for the nail – then press the plywood disc down onto it. Make sure the wooden O is in the centre of the plywood disc.

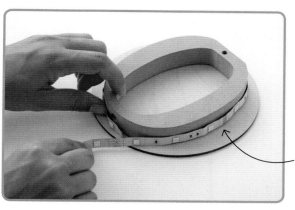

If the strip is so long it covers the hole, you'll be able to tidy it up with glue after step 25.

3 Beginning at the 8 mm (⁵⁄₁₆ in) hole, wrap the LED strip all the way around the wooden O to measure the length that you'll need. This is just to measure it – don't stick it down just yet.

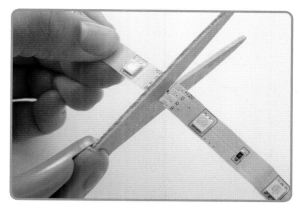

4 Cut the LED strip at the closest cut line nearest to the edge of the drilled hole. Only cut it at a cut line!

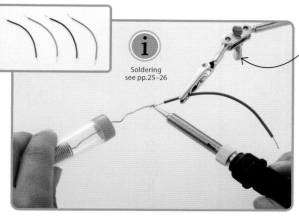

Soldering see pp.25–26

Use the third-hand tool to hold the wires steady as you apply solder.

5 Cut two black and two red wires each at 10 cm (4 in). Strip both ends of each wire, and tin one end of each wire. Set aside one black and one red wire until step 14.

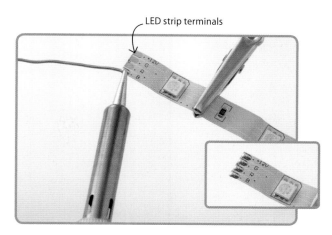

LED strip terminals

6 Apply a small blob of solder to each of the terminals on one end of the LED strip (yours may have two, three, or four). Make sure the blobs of solder do not touch.

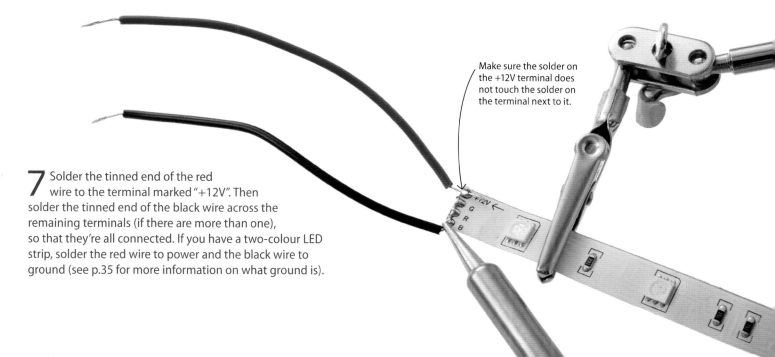

Make sure the solder on the +12V terminal does not touch the solder on the terminal next to it.

7 Solder the tinned end of the red wire to the terminal marked "+12V". Then solder the tinned end of the black wire across the remaining terminals (if there are more than one), so that they're all connected. If you have a two-colour LED strip, solder the red wire to power and the black wire to ground (see p.35 for more information on what ground is).

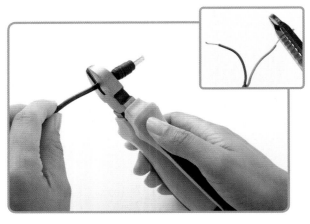

8 Making sure it is not plugged in, cut the jack off the end of the 12v AC/DC cable. Strip 3 cm (1⅛ in) of the outer insulation, then strip the ends of the internal wires.

9 Stick the decal onto the plywood disc using double-sided tape or glue. Neatly trim or fold over the edges if the decal is slightly larger than the disc.

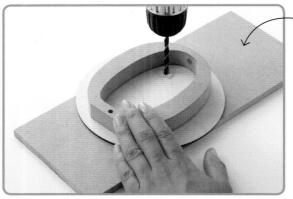

Use scrap wood to reduce the chance of damaging your furniture.

10 Drill a 5 mm (¹³⁄₆₄ in) hole through the plywood disc, off-centre but within the wooden O. Drill right through the decal. Try to choose a place that won't show too much on the decal design.

11 Feed the red and black wires connected to the LED strip into the wooden O through the hole in the bottom.

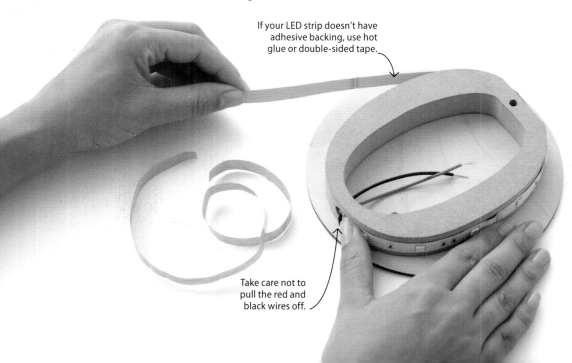

If your LED strip doesn't have adhesive backing, use hot glue or double-sided tape.

Take care not to pull the red and black wires off.

12 Remove the adhesive backing from the LED strip, and stick it to the outer edge of the wooden O. Make sure the red and black wires are near the edge of the hole.

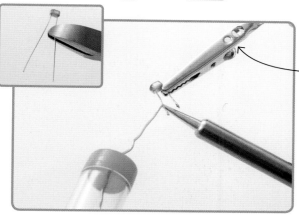

Use a third-hand tool to hold the photoresistor as you work.

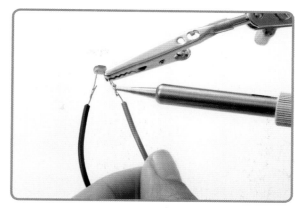

13 Use wire cutters to trim the legs of the photoresistor to a length of about 1 cm (⅜ in). Next, tin both legs with a little solder.

14 Solder the tinned ends of the red and black wires you prepared in step 5 to the legs of the photoresistor. It doesn't matter which one goes where.

15 Slip about 1 cm (⅜ in) of heat-shrink tubing over the ends of the wires, onto the soldered joints. Apply heat from the lighter, so that the tubing shrinks around the joints.

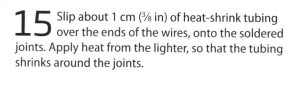

⚠ Always be careful when using an open flame.

The heat-shrink tubing will help to protect the connection.

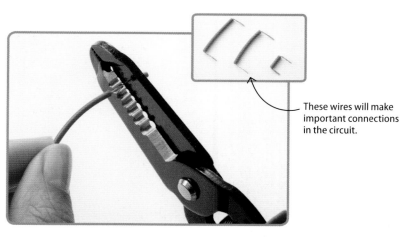

These wires will make important connections in the circuit.

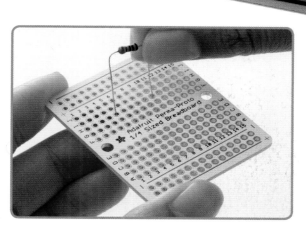

16 Cut three short wires – one 2 cm (¾ in) long and two 4 cm (1½ in) long. Strip each end of all three wires, using pliers to hold them if necessary, and then bend the ends down 90°.

17 Fold down the legs of the 10 kΩ resistor, and push them through terminals H5 and H10 of the breadboard.

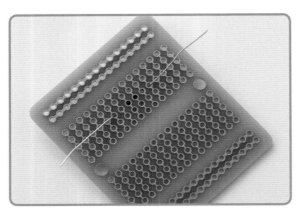

18 Turn over the breadboard, and bend the resistor's legs outwards to hold the resistor in place, ready for soldering.

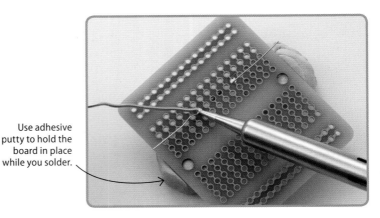

Use adhesive putty to hold the board in place while you solder.

19 Apply a small amount of solder around the resistor legs to secure them to the breadboard. To avoid short circuits, make sure no solder leaks onto the adjacent holes.

20 Following the breadboard map below, solder the second resistor, wire links, and transistors into the terminals of the board. Trim the excess wires and component legs from the underside of the board as you go.

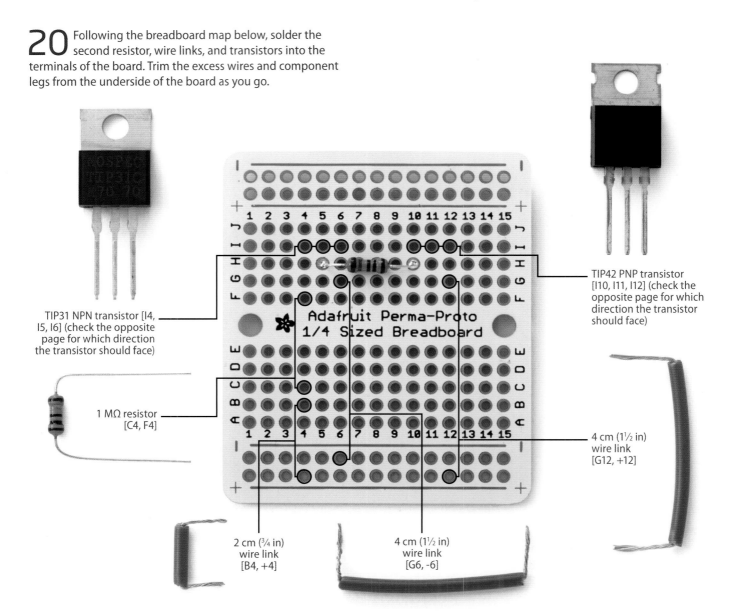

TIP31 NPN transistor [I4, I5, I6] (check the opposite page for which direction the transistor should face)

TIP42 PNP transistor [I10, I11, I12] (check the opposite page for which direction the transistor should face)

1 MΩ resistor [C4, F4]

4 cm (1½ in) wire link [G12, +12]

2 cm (¾ in) wire link [B4, +4]

4 cm (1½ in) wire link [G6, -6]

21 Next, take the wooden O and place the breadboard inside it. Feed the end of the power cord through the hole in the wooden O, so that it lies alongside the wires from the LED strip. Following the breadboard map below, solder the photoresistor wires, LED strip wires, and power wires onto the board.

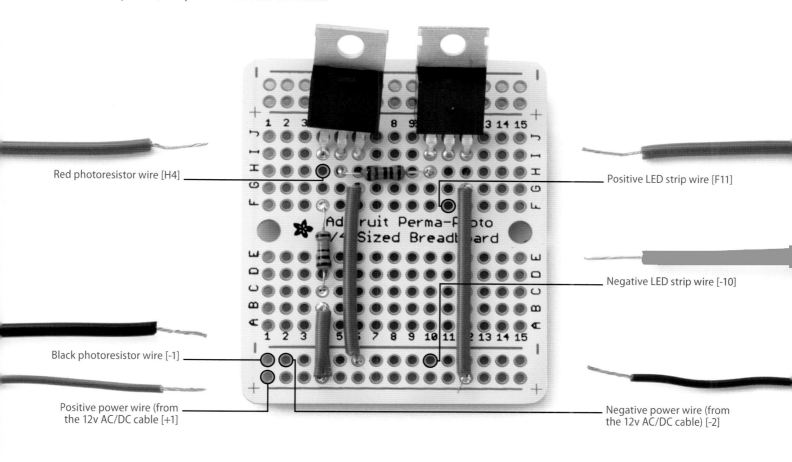

Red photoresistor wire [H4]

Positive LED strip wire [F11]

Negative LED strip wire [-10]

Black photoresistor wire [-1]

Positive power wire (from the 12v AC/DC cable [+1]

Negative power wire (from the 12v AC/DC cable) [-2]

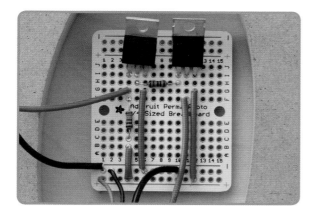

22 Once all of your components are soldered, your board should look like this. Plug the power adapter into a wall socket – the LED strip should not turn on.

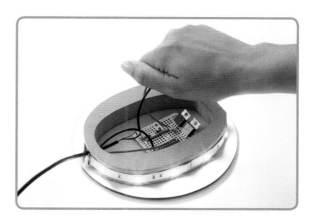

23 Now cover the photoresistor with your hand, so that very little light is falling on it. The LED strip should light up – if it doesn't, go back and check all of the connections are correct.

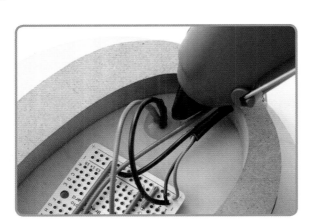

24 With the decal lying against the table, carefully push the photoresistor through the hole in the plywood disc, so that its flat surface is flush with the table. Now secure it in place with hot glue.

25 Apply hot glue to the hole in the end of the wooden O to secure the power cable and the wires from the LED in place.

26 Use hook-and-loop fasteners to secure the circuit onto the plywood disc inside the wooden O. Ask a friend to help you attach your night light to the wall, then plug in the power adapter and wait until it gets dark!

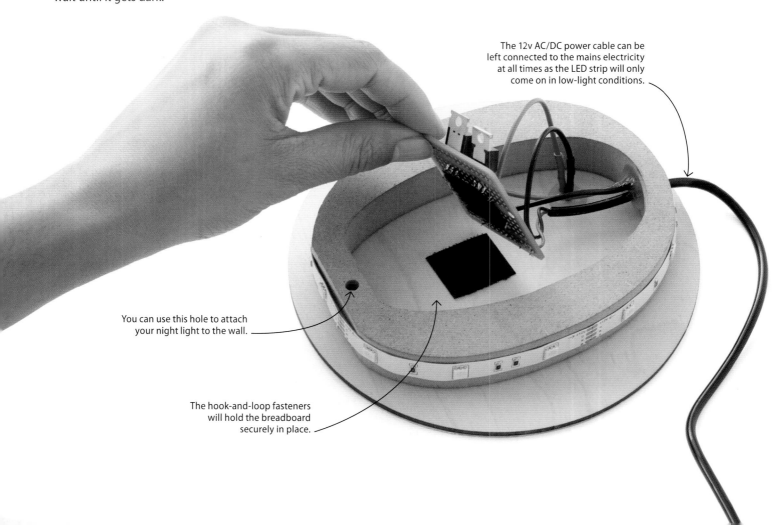

The 12v AC/DC power cable can be left connected to the mains electricity at all times as the LED strip will only come on in low-light conditions.

You can use this hole to attach your night light to the wall.

The hook-and-loop fasteners will hold the breadboard securely in place.

How it works

Electric current will always flow through the path of least resistance. The photoresistor opens a path for current during the day, but shuts it at night, causing the current to divert to the other parts of the circuit.

No current makes its way to the LED strip, so it is off.

Day

1. During the day, the photoresistor's resistance is low. This allows current from the mains to flow through it, and away from the other parts of the circuit. As it gets darker, the photoresistor's resistance increases, making it harder for current to flow through it. This leads to a chain reaction in the circuit.

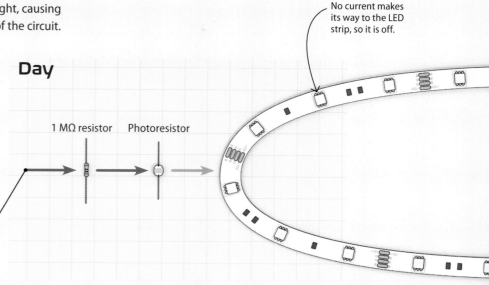

1 MΩ resistor   Photoresistor

The transistors act like switches in the circuit, but they also amplify the current when on.

2. Current cannot flow through the photoresistor. Instead, some current flows to the TIP31 transistor. This turns it on, and amplifies the current.

3. Some current then flows to the TIP42 transistor, turning it on, and amplifying the current again.

4. The path is then open, and the current has been amplified enough for it to flow through the LED strip, causing it to light up.

Night

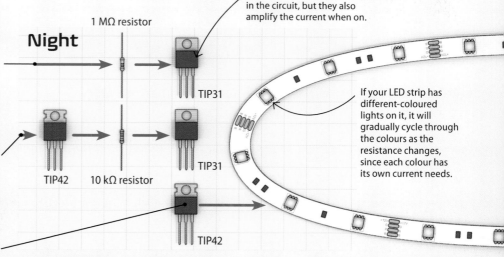

1 MΩ resistor

TIP31

TIP42   10 kΩ resistor   TIP31

TIP42

If your LED strip has different-coloured lights on it, it will gradually cycle through the colours as the resistance changes, since each colour has its own current needs.

Real-world inventions
Streetlights

The streetlights alongside roads are fitted with circuits like the one you have made – including the photoresistor. The lights remain off during the day, so they do not waste energy, and only come on at dusk as it begins to get dark. This is why they come on at slightly different times every evening.

Circuit diagrams

On these pages you will find the circuit diagrams for every project included in the book. These show how the components in each project are joined together by using simple images for each part of the circuit. Refer to p.33 for how circuit diagrams work.

ETC.

Coin battery
see pp.040–043

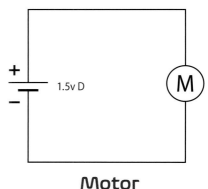

1.5v D

Motor
see pp.044–047

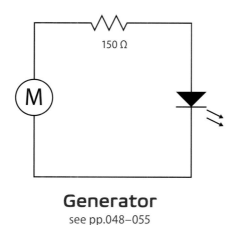

150 Ω

Generator
see pp.048–055

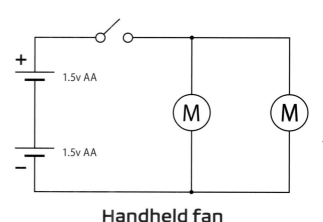

1.5v AA

1.5v AA

Handheld fan
see pp.056–59

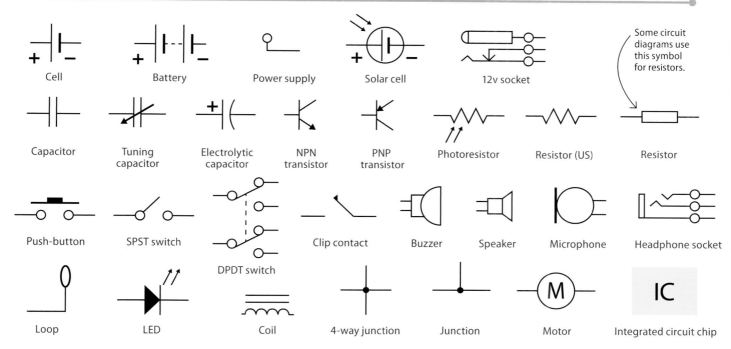

Cell	Battery	Power supply	Solar cell	12v socket	Some circuit diagrams use this symbol for resistors.
Capacitor	Tuning capacitor	Electrolytic capacitor	NPN transistor	PNP transistor	Photoresistor / Resistor (US) / Resistor
Push-button	SPST switch	DPDT switch	Clip contact	Buzzer	Speaker / Microphone / Headphone socket
Loop	LED	Coil	4-way junction	Junction	Motor / IC Integrated circuit chip

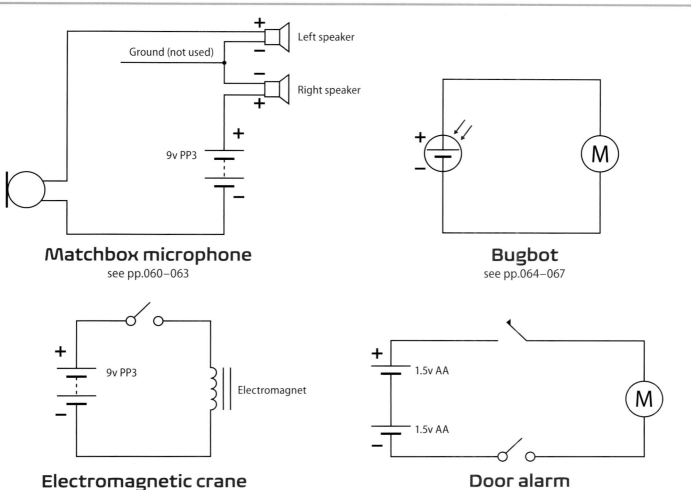

Left speaker

Ground (not used)

Right speaker

9v PP3

Matchbox microphone
see pp.060–063

Bugbot
Bugbot
see pp.064–067

9v PP3

Electromagnet

Electromagnetic crane
see pp.068–073

1.5v AA

1.5v AA

Door alarm
see pp.074–079

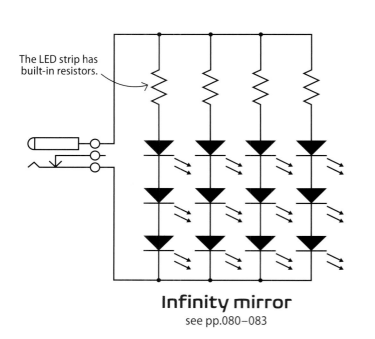

The LED strip has built-in resistors.

Infinity mirror
see pp.080–083

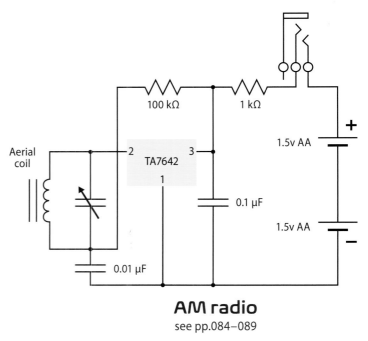

Aerial coil

100 kΩ   1 kΩ

1.5v AA

0.1 μF

1.5v AA

TA7642

0.01 μF

AM radio
see pp.084–089

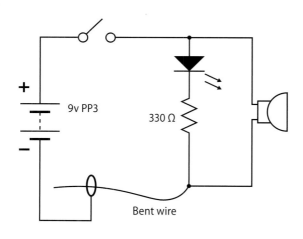

+ 9v PP3 −

330 Ω

Bent wire

Buzzer game
see pp.090–095

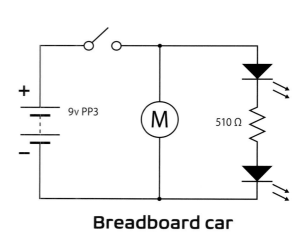

+ 9v PP3 −

M

510 Ω

Breadboard car
see pp.096–101

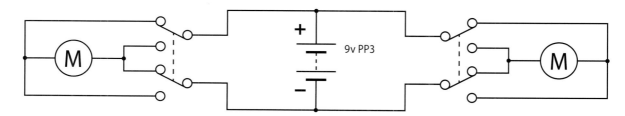

M

+ 9v PP3 −

M

Remote-controlled snake
see pp.102–111

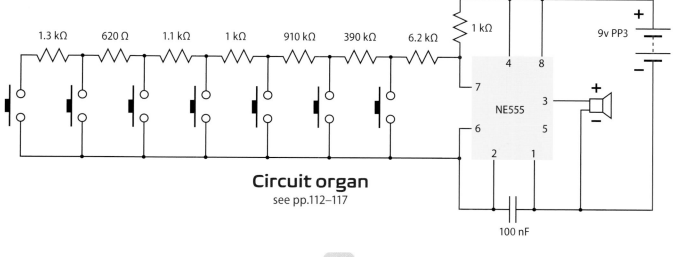

Circuit organ
see pp.112–117

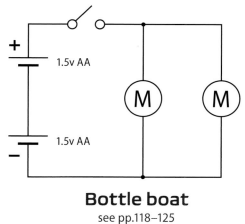

Bottle boat
see pp.118–125

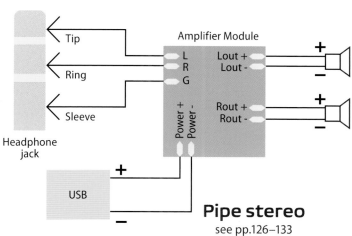

Pipe stereo
see pp.126–133

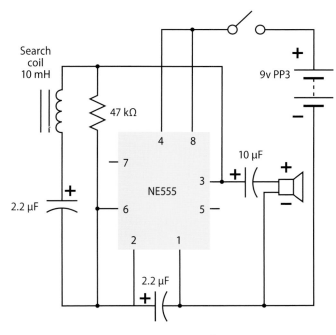

Ferrous metal sensor
see pp.134–141

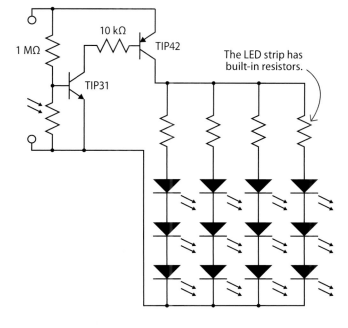

Automatic night light
see pp.142–151

Glossary

Alternating current (AC)
Electric current that repeatedly changes direction.

Ampere (A)
The unit of electric current, often shortened to "amp".

Amplifier
An electronic circuit that increases the amplitude of alternating currents. Amplifiers are normally used to make audio signals powerful enough to drive loudspeakers or headphones.

Amplitude modulation (AM)
"Amplitude" means the height of a wave, and "modulation" means to change something. AM radio stations take a base carrier wave and change its amplitude to carry sounds, which they then broadcast.

Anode
The part of any electrical device from which electrons leave. In a battery, this is the negative terminal.

Audio signal
An alternating current whose to-and-fro movement matches the vibrations carried by sound waves.

Axle
A rigid rod attached to one wheel or fixed between two wheels. The axle may turn with the wheels, or the wheels may turn around it.

Battery
A device that converts chemical energy into electrical energy through a chemical reaction. Batteries produce electrons, which can be used to create an electric current. Also called "cells".

Bradawl
A simple tool with a sharp point and a handle, used for making holes, or pilot holes to guide a drill bit when drilling.

Breadboard
A plastic board with holes and metal tracks that make it easy to assemble electronic circuits without the need for soldering. A perforated board is similar, but requires soldering.

Button switch
A type of switch that completes a circuit when you press it, but which contains a spring, so that the circuit opens again when you release it.

Capacitance
A measure of how much electric charge a capacitor can store. The unit of capacitance is the farad.

Capacitor
An electronic component, used in most electronic circuits, that stores electric charge. Most capacitors contain small metal plates separated by a small gap, coated in ceramic. *See also:* electrolytic capacitor.

Cathode
The part of any electrical device through which electrons enter. In a battery, this is the positive terminal.

Compact disc (CD)
A circle of plastic with aluminium on one side that carries music encoded digitally on a long spiral track.

Circuit
A path made of conductors – typically wires and electronic components – around which an electric current can flow.

Circuit diagram
A drawing that uses simple symbols to represent the wires and components in a circuit.

Coil
A long wire wound around many times.

Commutator
The part of an electric motor that transfers electric current from the motor's coils to its terminals.

Component
A small device used to control current or have some effect in an electric circuit. Examples include resistors, capacitors, and transistors.

Conductor
Any material that allows electric current to flow through it. Metals are very good conductors, while plastics and wood are not.

Conventional current
The name for electric current that involves the flow of positive electric charge. In electric circuits, it is negatively charged electrons that are moving, so the electron flow is opposite to conventional current.

Crocodile clip
A spring-loaded metal clip with jaws that hold on firmly to other objects. With wires soldered to them, they are often used to connect components in a circuit.

Current
See: electric current.

Cutting mat
A dense plastic mat that protects surfaces from sharp blades when cutting.

Digital
Anything represented by numbers (digits), specifically 0s and 1s. Inside computers, smartphones, and other digital devices, information is represented digitally.

Digital audio broadcasting (DAB)
A way of broadcasting that relies on computers to create the signals sent by the broadcaster.

Diode
An electronic component that allows electric current to flow through it in one direction only. A light-emitting diode (LED) produces light when current flows through it.

Direct current (DC)
Electric current that flows in one direction only.

Drill
A tool with a powerful motor that is used to make holes in materials such as wood, metal, and plastic.

Drill bit
A straight, sharp piece of metal that fits inside a drill to make holes in materials. Drill bits come in different sizes and for use with different materials.

Earphones
Small loudspeakers that fit inside a person's ears.

Electric charge
A basic property of electrons, protons, and other subatomic particles. Protons carry positive electric charge, while electrons carry negative charge. Charged particles attract or repel, depending on which kind of charge they carry.

Electric current
Any movement of electric charge. In electric circuits, it is the negatively charged electrons that move.

Electrical energy
Energy possessed by electrically charged particles, wherever there is a build-up of electric charge, or if charged particles are moving (in an electric current). In electric circuits, electrical energy can be transformed into other forms of energy, such as light or sound energy.

Electricity
A form of energy resulting from charged particles. Also used to mean the supply of electric current in a circuit.

Electrolyte
A substance that can conduct electric current. There is an electrolyte inside a battery.

Electrolytic capacitor
A capacitor that can store large amounts of electricity.

Electromagnet
A coil of wire wrapped around a piece of iron. When electric current flows through it, it produces a strong magnetic field.

Electromagnetism
The study of the link between electricity and magnetism.

Electromotive force (emf)
Any force that makes particles with electric charge move. In an electric circuit, a battery, solar cell, or a generator provides the emf, which makes electrons move around the circuit.

Electron
A tiny particle, several of which are found in each atom of matter. Electrons carry negative electric charge. They can break free from their atoms, and are then free to move around.

Enamel
In electronics, "enamelled wire" is copper wire coated with a red plastic that insulates the wire.

Energy
The ability to make things happen. Many different things have energy, including sound, light, and electricity, and energy can be transferred between them, such as when electrical energy produces sound energy in a loudspeaker.

Farad (F)
The unit of capacitance.

Ferrite rod
A solid cylinder made of a material (ferrite) that is rich in iron. Ferrite rods with coils of wire wrapped around them are used in some circuits, particularly amplitude-modulation radios.

Ferrous metal
Any metal or alloy (mixture of metals) that contains the element iron. The most common ferrous metal is steel.

Frequency
The rate at which something repeats, measured in units called hertz (Hz).

Frequency modulation (FM)
"Frequency" means the rate at which something repeats, and "modulation" means to change something. FM radio stations take a base carrier wave and change its frequency to carry sounds, which they then broadcast.

Galvanization
A process in which metallic items are coated with the element zinc. The zinc coating prevents the metal beneath from rusting.

Generator
A device with magnets and coils arranged around a shaft, that produces an electromotive force when the shaft is turned.

Ground
The part of an electric circuit with the lowest voltage. In battery-powered circuits, it is the battery's negative terminal.

Heat-shrink tubing
A plastic tube that shrinks when heat is applied to it. In electronics, it is used to coat metal parts with a layer that will not conduct electricity, to prevent short circuits.

Hot-glue gun
A handheld tool that has a heating element. The heat melts a solid glue stick, and the molten glue exits at the front of the tool.

Hydroelectricity
Any electricity whose energy comes from moving water.

Insulation
The coating on a wire, usually plastic. Insulation is made of an insulator – any material that does not allow electric current to pass through it.

Insulator
A material that does not allow electric current to flow through it. Plastic is a good insulator, and is used as the coating of wires so that current can only flow through the metal inside.

Integrated circuit (IC)
A complicated electric circuit whose components are embedded within a single piece of material, normally the element silicon. The silicon is housed in a plastic package with metal legs that allow it to be connected to a larger circuit.

Glossary

Iron
A very common metal. Steel is made of iron mixed with small amounts of other elements.

Jib
The part of a crane that holds the object to be lifted. Most jibs have a hook at the end.

Jumper wires
Small pieces of wire used to connect different parts of an electric circuit, especially circuits made on a breadboard.

Kinetic energy
The energy of anything that is moving.

LED strip
A plastic strip containing a row of light-emitting diodes.

Light-emitting diode (LED)
An electronic component that produces light when electric current flows through it. As with all diodes, current can only flow through it in one direction.

Loudspeaker
A device that turns electrical energy into sound energy.

Magnet
An object that produces a magnetic field. Permanent magnets have a magnetic field all the time, while the coil of an electromagnet has a magnetic field only when electric current flows through it.

Magnetic field
The area around a magnet or electromagnet, in which other magnets will be attracted or repelled.

Magnetic pole
One of the two opposite ends of a magnet, where the magnetic field is strongest. The poles are called north (N) and south (S).

Magnetism
Describes anything to do with magnets, but particularly the forces between any two magnets.

Mains electricity
Powerful electricity supplied to homes and businesses.

Metal
A solid material that is a good conductor of electricity.

Motor
A device that contains magnets and coils arranged around a shaft. When electric current flows through the coils, the shaft turns.

Multimeter
A tool that is used to measure voltages and electric currents in electric circuits, or to test electronic components.

Negative
Used to describe the kind of electric charge carried by electrons, but it also refers to any value less than zero.

Ohm (Ω)
The unit of resistance.

Oscillating
Describes something that moves back and forth.

Parallel circuit
An electric circuit or part of a circuit that splits into two or more branches. Each of the electrons moving through the circuit can only flow along one branch, so the electric current splits, too.

Photoresistor
An electronic component whose resistance changes depending on how much light is falling on it.

Piezo sounder
An electronic component that has a membrane inside that oscillates rapidly when electric current flows through it, so that it produces sound.

Pitch
How high or low a sound is. Pitch depends on the frequency of the oscillation of the object creating the sound.

Pliers
A tool with two metal arms hinged together, used for gripping small objects, bending wires, or squashing things together with great force.

Polarity
The property of having poles or being polar. Some components have positive and negative poles that affect how they behave in circuits.

Positive
Used to describe the kind of electric charge carried by protons, but it also refers to any value greater than zero.

Potentiometer
Another name for a variable resistor, which is a kind of electronic component whose resistance can be changed, normally by turning a knob. A potentiometer is used as the volume control of a radio.

Power
The amount of energy a device uses or produces every second. It is measured in units called watts (W).

Propeller
An object with curved blades that pushes against air or water when it spins.

Pulley
A device that has a grooved wheel that is free to spin. A rope or chain fits into the groove, and transmits forces between pulleys in different parts of a machine.

Radio
An electronic device that receives signals broadcast using radio waves. Radios decode the audio signals carried by the radio waves, so we can hear sounds broadcast from far away.

Radio wave
An invisible wave produced by a metal pole called an antenna, that travels extremely quickly, and can be used to carry information, such as music.

Remote control
A device with switches and other controls on it that can be used to control machines, toys, or electric circuits at a distance.

Resistance
A measure of how well a material or a component allows electric current to flow. The higher the resistance, the less current will flow.

Resistor
An electronic component with a fixed resistance. Resistors are used to control how much electric current flows in different parts of an electric circuit.

Series circuit
An electric circuit in which all the wires and components are connected one after the other, with no branches.

Short circuit
A path through which electric current can flow between two parts of a circuit that should not be directly connected. It is a fault in a circuit, and can make a circuit fail.

Solar panel
A device that produces an electromotive force when light shines on it.

Solder
An alloy (mixture of metals) with a melting point low enough that it melts when heated by the tip of a soldering iron. It is used to form solid joints that can conduct electricity.

Soldering iron
A tool with a tip that becomes hot enough to melt solder, used in connecting parts of electric circuits.

Solid-core wire
Wire coated with insulation, that has a single metal wire inside. The metal is strong enough to be pushed into breadboards, but thin enough to be cut easily.

Solution
A liquid with other compounds dissolved in it.

Sound wave
A wave produced by a vibrating object, which travels through the air as disturbances in air pressure. Loudspeakers, earphones, and piezo sounders produce sound waves.

Spring clamp
A tool for holding things firmly – particularly useful when sawing or drilling.

Steel
A material made of iron with small amounts of other elements mixed in.

Stereo
Describes an audio signal or an audio device with two "channels" – one for the right and one for the left.

Stranded wire
Wire coated with insulation, that has several thin metal strands inside. Stranded wire is easier to work with than a solid-core wire, but it is more difficult to plug into a breadboard.

Switch
An electronic component that allows electric current to flow, or stops it from flowing, through wires connected to its terminals.

Terminal
Any metal part of a battery or an electronic component that allows electric current to flow.

Third-hand tool
A useful tool with crocodile clips that can hold wires and electronic components steady while you solder them.

Torque
A turning force. An electric motor produces a torque that can turn a propeller or a drill bit.

Transistor
An electronic component that acts as an electronic switch, or an amplifier of current.

Universal Serial Bus (USB)
A technology used to connect, carry information between, and power electronic devices.

Variable capacitor
An electronic component – a type of capacitor whose capacitance can be varied, typically by turning a knob.

Vibration
A rapid motion to-and-fro used to describe the motion of solid objects. Vibrating objects produce sound waves.

Volt (V)
The unit of electromotive force (emf) or voltage.

Voltage
A measure of the electromotive force (emf) produced by a battery or generator, but also the amount of emf at any point of a circuit. Voltage is measured in volts (V).

Watt (W)
The unit of power.

Wire
A flexible length of thin metal, normally copper, used to connect different parts of an electric circuit. Most wires are coated in plastic insulation.

Wire cutters
Sharp-bladed tools like scissors but strong enough to cut through wires.

Wireless
Describes any electronic device that is connected to another device, but not by wires. A wireless network is a group of computers connected wirelessly, using radio waves.

Wire strippers
A tool used to strip the insulation off the ends of wires, to reveal the metal inside, making it possible to connect them to components or other wires when building an electric circuit.

Index

Acknowledgments

The publisher would like to thank the following people for their assistance in the preparation of this book:
Lee Barnett, Graham Baldwin and Nicola Torode for health and safety advice; Stephen Casey and Paddy Duncan for building, testing, and tweaking the projects; Adam Brackenbury and Steven Crozier for picture retouching; Kelsie Besaw, Alexandra Di Falco, Daksheeta Pattni, Anna Pond, and Samantha Richiardi for testing the projects; Xiao Lin, Anna Pond, Daksheeta Pattni, Melissa Sinclair, and Abi Wright for hand modelling; Emily Frisella for editorial assistance; Shahid Mahmood and Joe Scott for design assistance; Joshua Brookes for the "Circuit organ" project, and Techgenie for permission to use the "Remote-controlled snake" project; Helen Peters for the index; and Victoria Pyke for proofreading.

The publisher would like to thank the following for their kind permission to reproduce their photographs:
(Key: a-above; b-below/bottom; c-centre; f-far; l-left; r-right; t-top)

43 Science Photo Library: Royal Institution of Great Britain (bc). **55 Dreamstime.com:** Peter Dean (c). **59 Dreamstime.com:** Yocamon (clb). **63 Dreamstime.com:** Edward Olive (ca). **67 123RF.com:** Allan Swart (clb). **w73 Dreamstime.com:** Dan Van Den Broeke (bc). **79 Alamy Stock Photo:** Desintegrator (crb). **83 iStockphoto.com:** EvgeniyShkolenko (clb). **89 Alamy Stock Photo:** Realimage (tc). **95 Alamy Stock Photo:** Tim Savage (clb). **101 Solar Impulse Foundation:** (clb). **111 Dreamstime.com:** Akiyoko74 (bl). **117 Getty Images:** Andrew Lepley / Redferns (bc). **125 Alamy Stock Photo:** Newscom (crb). **133 iStockphoto.com:** arogant (c). **141 Dreamstime.com:** Mrreporter (bc). **142 NASA:** NASA, ESA, the Hubble Heritage Team (STScI / AURA), A. Nota (ESA / STScI), and the Westerlund 2 Science Team (cb). **143 NASA:** NASA, ESA, STScI, R. Gendler, and the Subaru Telescope (NAOJ) (ca). **144 NASA:** NASA, ESA, STScI, R. Gendler, and the Subaru Telescope (NAOJ) (cr). **146 NASA:** NASA, ESA, STScI, R. Gendler, and the Subaru Telescope (NAOJ) (tr). **151 Dreamstime.com:** Theendup (bc)

All other images © Dorling Kindersley
For further information see: www.dkimages.com